Honoring Death
The Arte of Daemonolatry
Necromancy

S. Connolly

Honoring Death
The Arte of Daemonolatry
Necromancy

S. Connolly

DB Publishing
United States of America

DB Publishing is an imprint of Darkerwood Publishing Group, PO Box 2011, Arvada, CO 80001. Contact the publisher for bulk purchases and discounts or contact ofs.admin@gmail.com for online wholesale purchase links.

Book Design by DB Publishing, Adrianna.
Cover Design: Adrianna
Editorial: B. Morlan

Contents

For Grandma
I told you that we would talk once you left
this world, and we have. You are missed
every day. With love, may you rest in peace.

&

For Lyra
As a necromancer you are the most talented
I've ever met. Thank you for helping me
when I needed it most. Your wisdom and
healing taught me so much. You are my
Alyssa (which is a compliment, indeed.)

Acknowledgements

Like usual a good number of people helped me with this book. A lot of folks offered input and even more sat around discussing necromancy with me. First, I want to thank my beta-readers who, as usual, were very thorough in their questions and comments and helped me to make this book more useful for my readers. As a writer and a longtime magician I sometimes take for granted that readers should know things they don't and my readers are kind enough to find those places for me so I can correct them. My thanks for this goes to Jeremy, Cory, and Ken. You guys are great!

I'd also like to thank B. Morlan for offering a great deal of input and allowing me to note some of his family traditions here. I'd also like to thank Lyra, Jace, Breanna, and Karen for sharing their experiences as necromantic magicians with me. You are all brilliant and very talented. You helped me grow a great deal as a necromancer in the past eight years. I am truly blessed.

And finally, I'd like to thank my editor, Brad, who painstakingly went over my manuscript, line edited and offered a great deal of input and suggestions to make this a better book. All writers need editors and I am grateful you're mine.

Warnings

The general rule about necromancy (i.e. raising the dead) is don't do it unless you absolutely have to and you know what you're doing. It's not something you really want to do for a "kick" or just to experiment. Of all the different types of magickal work out there, Necromancy is usually where people get themselves in trouble and end up with poltergeists and other haunting phenomena. So please use extreme caution when using this book or performing any ritual wherein you are contacting the spirits of deceased loved ones or the deceased in general. Sometimes "Others" (i.e. entities who were never human and who can be malevolent or mischievous) can fool the beginning necromancer into believing it is the deceased person they're seeking. This is the primary reason why Daemonolaters invoke Daemons of Death (and the death energy) into the ritual space - to filter out the riff raff. However - don't think this is a foolproof method or that it is any less dangerous. Some "Others" are cunning and devious and can find ways around certain safeguards. Always have a banishing/exorcism ritual handy after a work of true necromancy just in case.

I say true necromancy as not all Daemonolatry necromancy rites involve raising and speaking with the actual dead. Sometimes it's merely communing with the death energy on a subconscious or semi-conscious level and utilizing that to get a fresh start or to facilitate a spiritual rebirth or some sort of major life change from new babies to divorce and everything in between and not excluding the physical death of a loved one.

It's also important to point out that the dead should be treated with a great deal of respect. All rituals herein should be performed with the same respect you show for the Daemonic divine.

Also – beware of becoming emotionally or mentally dependent on necromantic divination or necromancy in general when it comes to making life decisions. This warning could extend to any type of divination or necromancy. Divination is a tool. Futures and outcomes can be changed because the future is not written in stone.

And finally, necromancy should not be performed by unstable individuals. A lot of people get angry with me for putting these warnings in my books but the truth is it's very important to understand that mentally unstable individuals have a higher chance of attracting negativity to them and higher chances of having a frightening experience. I can't stress enough that necromancy is not something to be trifled with lightly. Be healthy.

I am not responsible for what happens to anyone using this book. Nor do I make any guarantees or warranties in its publication. Perform the rites herein at your own discretion and at your own risk.

Death
By Emily Dickinson

Because I could not stop for Death,
He kindly stopped for me;
The carriage held but just ourselves
And Immortality.

We slowly drove, he knew no haste,
And I had put away
My labor, and my leisure too,
For his civility.

We passed the school, where children strove
At recess, in the ring;
We passed the fields of gazing grain,
We passed the setting sun.

Or rather, he passed us;
The dews grew quivering and chill,
For only gossamer my gown,
My tippet only tulle.

We paused before a house that seemed
A swelling of the ground;
The roof was scarcely visible,
The cornice but a mound.

Since then 'tis centuries, and yet each
Feels shorter than the day
I first surmised the horses' heads
Were toward eternity.

Dear Reader, I have included my favorite poem by Emily Dickinson since it is fitting for such a book. Please note I have printed this particular version (**with** the fourth stanza which is often edited out for whatever reason) because it would be incomplete otherwise. I do hope you'll take a moment to enjoy it before continuing.

The Arte of Necromancy

The third sister, Morgan le Fey, was put to scole in a nonnery, and ther she lerned so moche that she was a grete clerke of nygromancye.

-Malory, Sir Thomas d.1471
c.1470 Morte d'Arthur, bk.1, ch.2.

Necromancy is a topic that either draws the curious or repels those who fear death. It is something few people understand and even fewer practice. Well, actually necromancy is something that many people practice - they just refuse to call it necromancy because necromancy is a scary word.

Literally, the word means to communicate with the dead. It's taken on other connotations, however. Some believe Necromancers seek to bring the dead back from the grave, or to conjure the dead to hurt others. In a historical context, necromancy was a word often used in conjunction

S. Connolly

with anyone who allegedly practiced magick including witches and sorcerers of every ilk. Necromancy has often been used interchangeably with the word magic in general.

This is not the case. Most certainly those who practice the arte of magick in any form have come across necromancy and sure, numerous magicians have practiced necromancy. However, not all magicians are necromancers. Necromancers purposefully seek to commune with the dead for a reason; usually to impart hopeful or loving messages to the living (for comfort and consoling), to learn the outcome of a situation, or to come to better understand or accept death (including change). Just because one obsesses about death, listens to Goth music, hangs out in graveyards, or finds everything about death fascinating does not automatically make one a necromancer any more than owning or running a liquor store makes one an alcoholic.

I'm not going to start this book by giving you a history of different cultures' views of death. You can get that anywhere and I'd merely be researching and regurgitating information anyway. Suffice to say necromancy has been practiced throughout human history through every culture known to man. I'd much rather take a practical approach to necromancy by sharing personal experiences and giving you practical working knowledge.

First let me start at the beginning. When I was very young I would often see shadows and talk to people no one else could see. Those around me attributed it to an overactive imagination. I just thought I had secret friends who had powers of invisibility. But my true interest in necromancy began when I was eight years old. I remember growing up hearing fantastical family ghost stories about seeing and communicating with the dead. Necromancy has been a "gift" on the female side of our family for generations. Each generation has tales to impart. From my great grandmother seeing smoke pour out of a pair of boots at the end of the bed at the same time my great grandfather was dying in a barn fire, to my grandmother seeing the soul of her dead child leave the house at the child's exact moment of death, to my mom and aunt being visited by dark shadows, to me being visited by those same dark shadows and seeing the souls of dead things leave their bodies.

It was this last experience that caused me to begin checking out books about divination and necromancy from the school and local library at the tender age of twelve.

I haven't told a lot of people this story simply because I've always been very ashamed of myself. A lot happened during my teens and early twenties. A lot of it scared the shit out of me (pardon the expletive, but it's fitting). As a result of this for a lot of years I viewed my ability for necromancy as a curse. I was terrified to go into graveyards because I didn't know how to block out the energy or to quiet the voices of the dead. I couldn't handle it and quite frankly it terrified me. Seeing the dead was even worse. I pushed my luck with it though, even though it scared me, and finally by the time I was in my early twenties, after a great deal of paranormal investigating and scaring myself so badly - I completely blocked my ability out. I'm not even sure how I did it. But somehow I'd figured out how to effectively tune out the dead even though sometimes they would still get through with frightening consequences (stories which you'll read in this book when I have a point to illustrate).

Then, in the mid-nineties something happened. On October 31, on my way to a Euronymous rite, a black cat and a white cat ran in front of my car. I slammed on the brakes but it was too late. Sadly I hit both cats. I got out of my car in a panic, frantically searching for the injured animals in hopes I could get them to the cat hospital fifteen minutes away. Several other motorists who'd seen the incident stopped to help me look for them. We never did find the cats despite four of us searching for at least a half hour. I love animals and so for me – this was a traumatic experience. I'd killed another living thing. I went to the ritual with a heavy heart and grief stricken. That was the night the dead came back. And my abilities came back with a vengeance.

I began having vivid, morbid dreams about dead cats. Then dead dogs. Then dead people. Then dead people who I'd known when they were alive. They'd come back into my dreams and give me their final words. It was a terrible experience. I still shudder thinking about it. There were nights I'd wake up screaming from the dreams and the dreams wouldn't go away. The man who raped me as a girl would often come back into my dreams to apologize. Not only did I foresee my aunt's collapse from an aneurism, but after she died she came back to tell me not to feel guilty for not spending time with her (at the time I felt really bad about that). I saw murders that were committed locally only to wake up and see the paper the next morning. It was like living in a nightmare.

I tried working through the fear. I really did. I joined a local ghost hunting group and even went to investigate a graveyard. When I opened myself up, the fear crept in, past experiences came back to memory, and I immediately resigned as their medium. Later, the Demonolatry group I currently work with decided to do some paranormal investigations. I could never bring myself to go. When they'd bring back evidence, disembodied voices on digital voice recorders I'd feel myself go white because in my mind's eye, I could actually see the shadows of those the voices belonged to.

Finally deciding I needed to do something, I began talking to other necromancers. Much to my surprise, many of those I met had a similar story and assured me that my fear was very natural. It often is that way with necromancers who have a strong ability for it. The only exceptions seem to be those rare few who had someone to initially guide them through their "awakening" or those who may have the ability, but it's not strong or invasive. I have a strong and invasive mediumship ability that grows as I get older, which I'm told is how it works in our family. It's only been recently that I've been able to discuss the ability with my mother and sister. My mom told me she never discussed it with us because she didn't want to scare us. Of course we laughed when we all came clean with each other about having these experiences. Experiences we'd all been keeping to ourselves for fear people would think we were crazy.

What I'm most ashamed of is that *I* had the resources available to me to learn how to control and use my abilities and instead I turned my nose up at them and I ran from them. I was a stubborn woman in my twenties. It wasn't until I was in my thirties that I began working with Anpu (i.e. Anubis) to attune myself to the death energy and began working with Demonolatry necromancers to learn how to control my gift instead of allowing it to control me. I have learned a lot from them and I am writing this book in hopes of sharing this information with those of you who may be interested in the arte of necromancy or those of you who may be like I was – trying to figure out what's happening to you and how to control a gift that may seem like a curse.

S. Connolly

So now let me tell you what Demonolatry Necromancy means for me. Let me say first and foremost, necromancy is necromancy and isn't specific to any single tradition, Daemonolatry or other. But since I practice Demonolatry it's only right that I write the book from that perspective.

Demonolatry/Daemonolatry is the worship of Daemons, i.e. Divine Intelligences. Necromancy in this context not only includes working with the Daemons (i.e. Divine Intelligence) to communicate with the dead for divinatory or other reasons, but it also suggests working with the death Daemons and death energy. Communing with it. Not because you have a death wish or are suicidal, but rather to embrace death (i.e. learn to accept it as a part of physical existence or view it as an alchemical transformation), commune with the dead, and honor those who have passed before us.

This book will not require you to lurk in graveyards, dig up corpses, or carry dead things with you. Anyone who tells you that you must lurk in graveyards all the time or have a morbid fascination with death is likely more into gothic pop-culture or in love with the *thought* of being a necromancer rather than actually *being* one. Necromancers also aren't absolutely morose and depressed all the time. Most don't care to be surrounded by the sorrow of death twenty-four-seven. None of them act like necromancy doesn't come with a price. Now I'm sure there are exceptions to this, but I haven't met any.

I also won't tell you to procure or create a hand of glory, or tell you that you have to carry around human bones. You can pick up medieval grimoires for such things if you're interested in that. Also note that necromancy does not involve killing anyone or anything. My experience was unique and I've been told the ability for necromancy can occur to those who have had a near death experience as well as those who suffer trauma (which we'll discuss more later). A lot of the stereotypes about necromancy are just myths often perpetuated by the death fearing Abrahamic culture many of us are confined to.

You also won't find curses (execration) in this book. While certainly they have their place in necromancy, they really don't have a place in communing, working with, or honoring death or the dead. If you want curses and numerous, beautiful ways to get back at people you don't like, I suggest *The Daemonolater's Guide to Daemonic Magick*, or *The Complete Book of Demonolatry*. Both of which are more than adequate texts capable of teaching you how to exact magickal revenge.

Instead, what you'll find in this book are methods and recipes to help you commune with the Daemons of death, learn to accept change (i.e. metaphoric death), help you come to terms with death, methods for honoring those who have died, and yes - methods to communicate with the dead using divination.

I do believe you do need to have some natural talent as a medium to actually excel as a Necromancer, however since I also believe most people are, in the very least, clairsentient to some degree, I think you can still train yourself to commune with the Death energy and also "feel" the dead, even if speaking with them or seeing them seems beyond your grasp (for a rare few it is). So basically - it is the natural mediums among you who are going to benefit most from this book.

Mediums are able to:

1. See or feel the dead.
2. Speak with or communicate with the Dead.

We call them mediums because they are mediators between the living and the dead. A conduit, if you will, that can break through the veil to the other side. There are several ways by which a person often comes by their talents as a medium.

A. Some people are just born with it and don't remember a time when they weren't speaking to or seeing the dead.

B. Some mediums may seem psychic. Being especially Clairvoyant, Clairsentient, or Clairaudient heightens the chance that you not only have mediumship abilities, but also suggests that you will likely be able to hone and perfect those abilities.

C. Some people may have an experience here or there and then, as time goes on, the ability gets stronger (i.e. the dead begin to speak to them more often).

D. Sometimes the ability is triggered by a traumatic event (death in the family etc...)

I have run across numerous self-professed Necromancers in my time and I've noticed a trait among the more learned ones. These people, once they've come to understand their gifts and learn there's nothing to fear, usually don't have the same fear of death, nor do they experience the same level of loss or sadness when someone they love dies because they already KNOW what's on the other side.

Being a Medium:

All highly successful necromancers are mediums. Some people will tell you this isn't true, but from my direct experience there is no way around this. The good news is that most everyone has some form of mediumship talent, though sometimes in miniscule amounts. Sadly, some people are more attuned to their mediumship ability than others. You'll likely have a great deal of success as a Necromancer if you've experienced the following:

1. You've seen a spirit leave a dying body.
2. You've spoken to the dead (and/or they've spoken to you).
3. You find it very easy to attune yourself to the death energy.

Now this doesn't mean you see the dead around every corner. Nor does it mean you're like the women on TV shows like "Medium" or "Ghost Whisperer". Different people will have differing degrees of talent and the talent for Necromancy may show up in different ways based on the person and their unique way of communicating with and seeing the dead. There are no right or wrong answers here or one true way or anything like that. Some people will mostly see and speak with the dead in dreams. Others will hear them. Others still will see and hear them. Some people will merely "feel" them. Some may have varying levels of all these different forms of communication. Some may get their messages through "signs". Oftentimes strong mediumship abilities run in families (suggesting a genetic predisposition) and oftentimes the strongest mediums are female just because women are brought up to be in tune with their emotions, intuition and empathy whereas men are often forced, by society, to bury and ignore these things. The more sensitive

S. Connolly

the person, the more apt they are to be open to the supernatural. Don't take this to mean men can't be necromancers. They can and the men I've met who are successful necromancers are very talented at what they do. It's just that largely I meet more talented female necromancers than I do men. I don't know why this is, it just is. Also, necromantic abilities may develop and get stronger with age. This has certainly been my case, but I've also known necromancers who have had a strong ability since youth.

When can necromancy be performed?

Some believe the most potent necromancy can only be performed when the veil is thinnest. When is the Veil thinnest? Some will tell you around three AM. Many will tell you the veil between the worlds of the living and dead is thinnest on Halloween, which is partially true. The reality is that it's actually "around" Halloween but not necessarily on Halloween. In truth the veil is actually thinnest based on the day when Scorpio's influence is strongest (during the time when the sun is in Scorpio) and the actual timing of this influence changes from year to year. Why? Because Scorpio is often thought to be the sign closest to death and the denizens of the underworld. Scorpio is also the sage of the water signs and those who bear it are often psychic by their very nature. Now this is according to Western Astrology and doesn't take into account sidereal astrology which is a different ball of wax. Regardless, a necromancer is a necromancer and most talented necromancers don't need a thin veil to work with. If you do need a thin veil to work with, time your work after midnight or between October 31 and November 17 and you'll likely find yourself in a good position for successful work.

Some other considerations may include planetary influence. Saturn and Mars are traditionally planets ruling over death and therefore their hours, scents, and times of influence can also be used to work necromancy.

Finally, I think I need to address those who aren't theists per se. Those people who don't believe in life after death and who use magick strictly as a method by which to transform the self and the psyche. There is something for you in this book. Working with the death energy (and Daemonic Death archetypes) can help you attune to change, heal after loss, and transform yourself into a person who is malleable in the face of adversity. Remember that in the tarot deck the death card often signifies a major life change. Also, the divination section will be useful to anyone whether you believe in an afterlife or not. Remember that divination is just a tool.

Death & Daemonolatry

"I'm setting twenty-two tables for the funeral feast, Satan is by far the kindest beast..."

-Spiritual Cramp; Christian Death

First I'd like to say a few things about death. Death is something many of us have been taught to fear or think of as "unnatural". We avoid it even when it's inevitable as evidenced by our need to keep the terminally ill alive and suffering for as long as possible, even after they've lost consciousness. I've heard people at funerals talk about how they never expected the deceased to die. Or that the person died too young.

Here's my take on this - first, death is natural. If no one died, we'd be in a world of hurt. The world would be even more overpopulated than it already is. There is nothing "unnatural" about death. Sure, maybe the circumstances of death are sometimes unnatural. But the process of dying itself is just another part of the cycle of life. Birth, life, death - repeat.

Next, death does not discriminate - all living things are going to eventually die. None of us, healthy or sick, young or old, are guaranteed another day. It's something we need to learn to accept from a young age, but often aren't taught. It's only the manner of death and the time of death that are mysterious.

And finally, death itself is nothing to fear. It seems it's the *manner* of death that we really fear. After all, we'd all like a quick and painless death. Not to mention none of us wants to deal with the pain of loss of a loved one.

Death impacts the living more than the dead. That's why they (the infamous they) say that funerals are for the living, not the dead. Death is a painful loss for those left alive most certainly. Losing someone close to you or who you love deeply is like losing a part of yourself. It leaves a hole that will eventually heal in time, but there will always be a scar. It is because of these latter things (and the natural human ability for clairsentience, clairaudience, and clairvoyance) that necromancy came about to begin with.

There is another side of death, however. One that many people don't consider. Death is change. It is loss. Metaphoric *death* can be just as life altering as physical death for the person who lives through it. So in Daemonolatry, necromantic practices can, and often do, include rituals to accept other kinds of death including but not limited to: divorce, death of a career, loss of self-identity (mid-life crisis), loss of financial stability/home, etc...

Why Work With the Daemonic for Necromancy?

Because for some people the Daemonic helps to amplify the voices of the dead. This is a good thing for those whose mediumship ability isn't very strong. Daemonic energy can also help to filter out excesses and teach the necromancer focus (which is why I often employ Daemonic help to work with the dead). There are numerous Death Daemons you can work with and you'll find an entire chapter about them just ahead. To give you a quick list, Hades, Hecate, Thanatos, Eurynomous, Baalberith, Babael, Gamigin, Bune, Beleth, Mephisto, Bifrons, Murmur, Belial and Anubis. These are certainly not all of them.

The best way to find out which Daemons you work best with is to work with them. I find meditating on a Daemon's sigil or seal is very helpful. You'll find all the *base* information on the more popular Death Daemons on the following pages. Remember that Daemons often appear to the practitioner as we need them to appear as opposed to how others see them. The Daemon that appears male to you may be feminine to someone else etc... And I don't necessarily mean physical appearance, but rather "feel". Not only that – the purposes I've listed may not be all they preside over. The best way to learn the wisdom any Daemon has to impart is to work with that Daemon. They are the best teachers after all.

Death Daemons

There are scores of Death Daemons available for the practicing Daemonolater to work with. The Dukanté hierarchy has an entire family of them. The Goetic Hierarchy has them, too. These are the two hierarchies we'll work with in this book. I'll also be mentioning Anubis from Khemetic Daemonolatry because I have found Anubis to be a very powerful Daemon with regard to learning about the nature of death and learning to weather change. Don't forget the ancient Egyptians were really into their death rituals. Also note that I have not included all of your possible choices here. **Hades** and gods of other pantheons can also be worked with. One necromancer I know works with **Thanatos** who is a guide for the dead. So don't feel limited by the Daemons I've chosen to include in this book.

Eurynomous

Color: Black
Base Incense: Mullein
Metal: Silver
Planet: Mercury
Element: Earth
Direction: Northeast
Enn: *Ayar Secore on ca Eurynomous*
Date: October 31- November 2

Original Purpose: Daemon of Death, invoked for new beginnings, rebirth, the celebration of death, or to honor the dead.

Author's Notes: Eurynomous (also Euronymous) carries presence with him. When invoked he brings with him the shades that can cause some disorientation for the magician. Do not approach Eurynomous forthright. Sit back and become accustomed to his energy at first before directly approaching him. He is very helpful and has much wisdom to offer and much comfort to give a grieving magician. Expect to feel, at some point, a sense of loving calm in his presence..

Baalberith

Color: Black and Gray
Base Incense: Mandrake, Solomon's Seal and Mullein
Metal: Copper
Planet: Saturn
Element: Earth
Direction: North
Enn: *Avage Secoré on ca Baalberith*
Date: October 31- November 2

Original Purpose: Prince of dying. Rebirth and the protection of the dead on their passage.

Author's Notes: Also Ba'alberith and Balberith (some say also Berith). Baalberith can bring joy to the living after a loved one has passed. He is not as solid and calming as Eurynomous. He is an excellent Daemon to work with for communication with the dead as he'll gladly give magicians who prefer more active necromancy sessions the energy they need to facilitate that.

Babael

Color: Gray
Base Incense: Sage and Myrrh
Metal: Silver
Planet: Mercury
Element: Earth
Direction: All
Enn: *Alan Secore on ca Babeal*
Date: October 31- November 2

Original Purpose: Keeper of graves and protector of cemeteries. Also rebirth.

Author's Notes: Also Babael, Ba'al, and some say Ba'el. Babael can be invoked to protect any resting place of the dead (from vandals for example) as well as to keep the dead confined to a particular space. His energy is calming much like Eurynomous' but not as heavy. It's lighter and good for concealment.

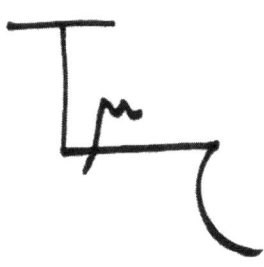

Mephisto

Color: Black
Base Incense: Frankincense and Mandrake
Metal: Silver
Planet: Mars
Element: Watery Part of Earth
Direction: Northwest
Enn: *Mesphito ramec viasa on ca*
Date: November 4 -17

Original Purpose: Keeper of the book of death. He keeps knowledge and secrets about necromancy and other sorceries.

Author's Notes: I've always worked with Mephisto as an execration Daemon, but he certainly isn't this limited. To foresee death, this is the Daemon to work with. His energy is flowing and encompassing and sometimes can be difficult to direct. I suggest drawing his energy into a wand via pillar rite and then using the wand to direct the energy.

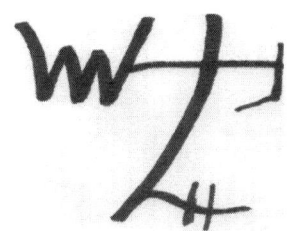

Beleth

KING

Color: Yellow
Base Incense: Frankincense
Metal: Gold
Planet: Sun
Element: Earth
Enn: *Lirach tasa vefa wehlc Beleth*
Date: July 22 – August 1

Original Purpose: Beleth is described as terrifying and it is said the magician must keep a hazel wand at the ready to keep Beleth's fury and flaming breath at bay. Causes love and desire.

Author's Notes: He is sometimes known as Bolfri by necromancers. Seek Beleth after death of a loved one to find stability and comfort. Beleth can help bring loved ones forward from the other side. Be careful of doing this unless absolutely necessary. An alchemists Daemon, he is a good Daemon to utilize when charging your necromantic incenses and oils using a pillar rite.

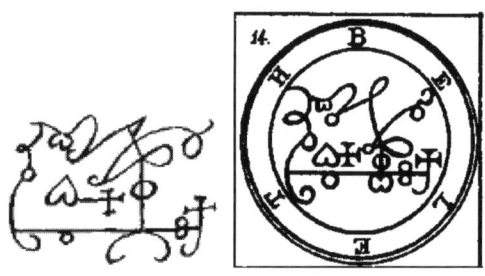

Bune

DUKE

Color: Green
Base Incense: Sandalwood
Metal: Copper
Planet: Venus
Element: Earth
Enn: (also Bime) – *Wehlc melan avage Bune Tasa*
Date: December 3 - 12

Original Purpose: He gives truthful answers, he can part the veil between the living and the dead and gather the dead. He can give riches and make a magician wise and well-spoken.

Author's Notes: Bune is one of the Goetia's biggest Necromancy Daemons. If you have a medium ready to channel the dead, invoke Bune to keep order and peace during the séance. He can impart understanding and wisdom about the nature of death as well.

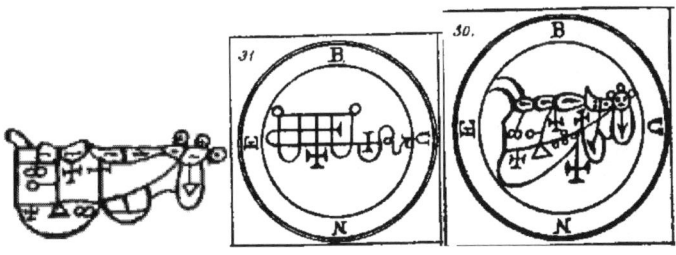

Bifrons

EARL

Color: Red
Base Incense: Dragon's Blood
Metal: Copper or Silver
Planet: Mars
Element: Earth
Enn: *Avage secore Bifrons remie tasa*
Date: June 21 – July 1

Original Purpose: Lights candles on the graves of the dead and can invoke the dead. He can make a man knowledgeable in astronomy and other sciences. He can teach the properties of stones and woods.

Author's Notes: Another Necromancy Daemon of Goetia. Work with Bifrons to communicate with the dead. This would be the Daemon invoked for a funeral ceremony to help usher the dead on their journey. Also invoke during rituals to honor ancestors or to learn to accept death.

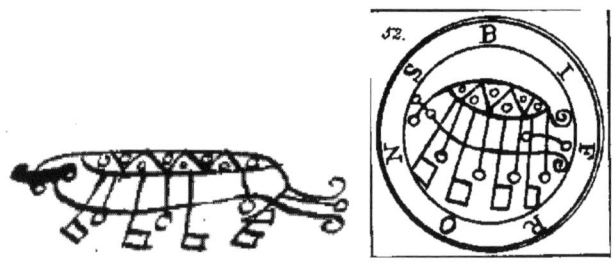

Gamigin

MARQUIS

Color: Violet
Base Incense: Jasmine
Metal: Silver
Planet: Moon
Element: Water
Enn: *Esta ta et tasa Gamigin*
Date: April 21 - 30

Original Purpose: Liberal Sciences and Speaking to dead sinners

Author's Notes: Also Samigina. Necromancy (to speak with any spirits of the dead). She can also help the necromancer by boosting or amplifying his ability as well as offer wisdom in the art of necromancy.

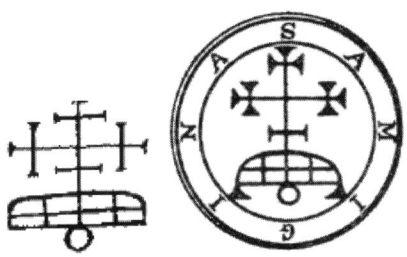

Murmur

DUKE

Color: Green
Base Incense: Sandalwood
Metal: Copper
Planet: Venus
Element: Water Fire
Enn: (also Murmus)- *Vefa mena Murmur ayer*
Date: September 12 - 22

Original Purpose: (Also an Earl) Teaches philosophy and can be invoked for necromancy.

Author's Notes: Murmur can keep the dead from harming the living or overstaying its welcome in possessing a medium during channeling sessions. Murmur, for me, was one of the more aggressive and intimidating necromantic Daemons of the Goetia.

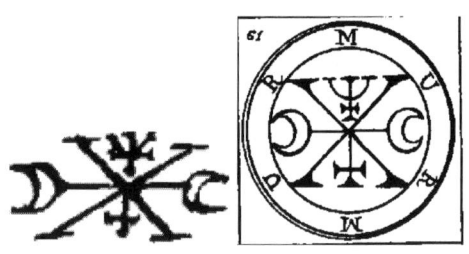

Belial

KING

Color: Yellow
Base Incense: Frankincense
Metal: Gold
Planet: Sun
Element: Fire (Earth)
Enn: *Lirach Tasa Vefa Wehlc Belial*
Date: January 30 – February 8

Original Purpose: Distributes titles and can make friends and enemies favor your position. He gives familiars. The magician must give offerings, sacrifices, and gifts if he wants Belial to be truthful.

Author's Notes: In the Dukante hierarchy, Belial is seen as the representative Daemonic force of earth. In this aspect, he is the destructive earth force. This makes invoking this aspect apt for necromancy.

.

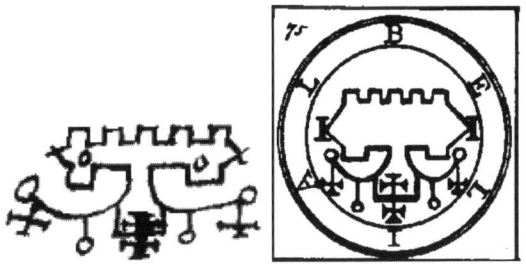

Hecate

Color: Black and Purple
Base Incense: Belladonna or Moon Flower
Metal: Mercury and Silver
Planet: Saturn/Mercury/Moon
Element: Fifth
Enn: *Anana Hecate Ayer At*
Date: Mid-Summer and October 30-November 2

Original Purpose: Greco-Roman triple goddess of magic and the crossroads. Hecate is also associated with the underworld and conjuring and speaking with the dead.

Author's Notes: (also Hekate and Hekat) Hecate, while an overall Daemon suitable for many tasks and guidance in most areas, is helpful to the necromancer not only in standard necromantic ways, but can also help the necromancer strengthen his/her abilities for necromantic work.

Anubis

Color: Yellow and Blue
Base Incense: Frankincense and Myrrh
Metal: Gold
Planet: Sun
Element: Fire part of Earth
Enn: *Nyana an ca Lirac meso Anubis*
Date: All

Original Purpose: Egyptian God of the afterlife. A funerary Daemon often employed for the Rites of Death. Gives safe passage (of the dead to the afterlife).

Author's Notes: (also **Anup, Anubis**, and **Ienpw)** I have successfully worked with Anubis to work through my fears of change and my fear of my necromantic abilities. Anubis' energy is comforting like that of Eurynomous, but possesses a lighter feel to it. There's more of a compassionate and empathic quality to it. That's the best way I can describe it.

.

Near Death Experiences

Out of the jaws of death.
Shakespeare, ***Twelfth Night, Act III, Sc. IV***

Many people become interested in Necromancy after having a near death experience. Many who have had such an experience will often feel like they've been "beyond the veil" and have a closer connection. It's true that near death experiences can sometimes trigger something in a person to make them closer to the death current, but don't think you have to have had a near death experience to be a necromancer. Abilities for necromancy can be triggered by other powerful events such as being involved in an accident or sudden situation where someone else died (human or animal), being present during the death of someone close to you, or you might just have a natural ability.

I have had a near death experience, but for me it didn't trigger what I already had. I think what I remember most was the feeling of hovering and then seeing the brightest light and feeling drawn to it, but it was like I was still tethered to my body. Different people have different experiences near death or if they die and are brought back. Scientists will tell you the bright light and the detached feeling is the brain struggling for oxygen at the time of death.

At most I can only tell you that my near death experience happened during my "blocking" period. And while it didn't scare me per se, it did make me more curious about it all. I sometimes think that if I hadn't had the experiences I've had I would have never gotten over the fear, I wouldn't have struggled to overcome the fear, and I wouldn't be writing this book.

How about you? What did your near death experience do for you? I posed this question to numerous necromancers with whom I spoke about this book and many of them say that their near death experience made them a better necromancer because they felt it made them feel closer to those who had passed. It made them feel more comfortable "walking" through the veil.

Dealing With Death

*Men fear death as children fear to go in the dark; and as that natural
fear in children is increased with tales, so is the other.*

-Bacon, Francis,Viscount St Albans
Essays, no.2,'Of Death'.

Dealing with the Pain and Loss of Literal Death

Since necromancers deal with death, they are, in
many cultures, the people sought out when someone of
their faith loses someone. So it's probably vitally important
that the necromancer understand grief and how to counsel
and help others through grief. Some necromancers may
find it easier to deal with the dead than the living, but
understanding grief can really go a long way to dealing
with those who have suffered a loss, and can make the
necromancer's job that much easier.

The stages of grief

Even necromancers experience grief. Now granted death doesn't usually destroy the necromancer. After all, people who are genuinely necromancers know for a fact that there is something beyond the physical world. We've seen it and some have even been there, however briefly. According to grief counselors there are 7 stages to the grieving process.

1. SHOCK & DENIAL-

This usually manifests in numbness and disbelief. You may feel like you're living in unreality or that everything is surreal. It can last for weeks.

2. PAIN & GUILT-

Once you get over the numbness you'll begin to feel pain. Sometimes the pain is intense and life altering. It's really important to let that pain out and allow for it and not try to hide from it by using drugs or alcohol (which sometimes people do when they can't deal with it.) There may also be feelings of guilt as you try to pin some blame on yourself or regret for all the things you should have, could have, would have done. Most people say this is the chaos period of grief.

3. ANGER & BARGAINING-

This is the point where many folks will start looking for someone or something to blame for the death of a loved one, or failure in a job or relationship, or loss of financial stability or whatnot. Oftentimes this anger and blame is unwarranted and is a direct result of the pain. We tend to think we can lessen our pain by finding someone or something to blame for the loss.

Others go through what is known as bargaining where the person may ask, "Why me?" and implore their higher power for a second chance like, "I promise I'll be a good person if you just bring my loved one back to me."

4. "DEPRESSION", REFLECTION, LONELINESS-

Sadness and reflection are normal in the process of grief. Some people may try to talk the depressed person out of it. This doesn't really apply. It's also normal to feel lonely or to feel like something is missing from your life. After my grandmother passed, there was a hole in my life that I was reminded of every Wednesday night (which was when I'd visit my grandmother). When you have a long-standing routine involving the person who has passed it is natural to feel like something is missing or to not know what to do with yourself. Many people may also feel the need to isolate themselves. Sometimes it's best to let this stage run its course.

5. THE UPWARD TURN-

This is the point where a person's depression, loneliness etc.. begins to lift. It's not a complete rebound, mind you, but the grieving person may feel like going out with friends or might laugh a little more. We have to remember that losing a loved one is rough and if you were close to that person and saw them frequently, or lived with them, you have to rebuild your life, change routines, and adjust to living without that person. This is often easier said than done.

6. RECONSTRUCTION & WORKING THROUGH-

Once the grieving person has finally started to re-adjust to the change and loss, they can begin rebuilding and reorganizing their life and will find it easier to tackle problems such as financial situations etc...

7. ACCEPTANCE & HOPE-

The final stage of grief is when the grieving person comes to accept the reality that their loved one is gone. Never expect instant happiness during this stage. Happiness is a gradual thing as the person realizes that (s)he does and can exist without the loved one and that life must go on. Also, the pain of loss never really heals - it often just lessens with time as we grow more accepting of our circumstances.

The Literal Death

Old Age

Even when a loved one is advanced in age and nearing the twilight years does not make the acceptance of death any less painful. Perhaps easier to accept (as the person who isn't dying), yes, but not less painful. Loss is loss regardless the age of the person who passed. We can never assume a person shouldn't feel loss just because their mother was ninety-three when she passed. Sure, her death was inevitable, but so is all death.

Illness

Many say that death after an extended illness (such as cancer) is a blessing. While this may be true that those left behind are happy their loved one is no longer suffering (or there may be a sense of relief there), they are still going to feel great sadness and loss. Nothing can prepare you for the death of a loved one even when they're dying.

Sudden & Unexpected Death

Sudden and unexpected deaths often cause the most problems not only for the spirit of the deceased, but also for the living people left behind. Often you'll find that in cases where spirits are hanging around in this world, grounded, they often had a traumatic death circumstance or they weren't ready to die. Or they simply have something in this world keeping them here. My grandmother had promised my nephew that she would be there for his high school graduation, and seems to have been sticking around for that. Occasionally I'll have dreams about her telling me to come visit her as well (her gravesite). So I know she's sticking around to keep her promise to my nephew. On the other hand, some people pass and move on without problems. This all brings about the question - how does a necromancer help cross a spirit over?

Crossing Spirits Over

We see in the movies necromancers merely reasoning with the spirit and getting them to pass. Many necromancers will tell you that, yes, sometimes it can work that way provided the spirit is not confused or enraged. Here's the problem with that simplistic viewpoint as I see it (and feel free to disagree) - most often the spirits that are grounded are confused or enraged or have unfinished business and that's why they're sticking around to begin with. This means that either you need to help the spirit out (if you can reasonably do so - sometimes you may find you can't) or you may need to cross them over by opening a gate for them.

Gate opening is a complex process and anyone who isn't a natural gatekeeper and tells you they can open a gate easily is probably pulling your leg. I'm sure there are exceptions. Opening gates can be dangerous. It takes time and energy, and can produce dramatic results. See "Parting the Veil" later in this book for information on how this is accomplished.

In the case of nasty human spirits or "others", you may have to have them forcibly removed by Daemonic intervention. (Crossings and exorcism rituals are included in the ritual section of this book.)

Dealing with Metaphorical Death

Metaphoric death comes in many forms. It is the dramatic life changes that cause stress and anxiety in the average human. This can include the loss of a job or career, a divorce, or a loss of independence or one's home. The beauty of a metaphoric death (or change) is that it is often followed be a rebirth and an awakening. Like the Phoenix, one rises from the flames of destruction.

While the physical loss of a loved one is difficult, never underestimate the pain, loss and suffering experienced by a person going through a divorce, a couple who can't have children, or the fifty-year-old man who loses his job only to discover his skill set is obsolete and his purpose in life, his career, his reason for being for so long has been taken from him. Or what about the person whose independence is taken away by a debilitating disease or advancing age, or whose memories are lost to Alzheimer's.

These are all examples of life altering changes that can cause a metaphoric death.

It's scientifically proven that these life changes can trigger the same stages of grief in the person suffering the loss. Humans are creatures of habit. Some of us weather change better than others, but everyone has to try to keep their balance when it comes to the metaphoric death. Use coping rituals (found later in this book) meant to imbue the body and mind with internal strength to deal with these difficult changes. Like always, a strong support system is key to any person's success. For the necromancer this is no different. Working with the death energy can only take you so far. As a physical, social being, you will find yourself needing human contact and compassion regardless the Daemonic intervention. I suggest working with Anubis, Eurynomous or Bune during change rituals. Of course you may work with whichever Daemonic forces you wish to work with based on comfort and your personal relationship with any particular Daemon. Keep that in mind for all the rituals in the ritual section of this book.

Honoring the Dead

To-morrow, and to-morrow, and to-morrow,
Creeps in this petty pace from day to day,
To the last syllable of recorded time;
And all our yesterdays have lighted fools
The way to dusty death. Out, out, brief candle!
Life's but a walking shadow

Shakespeare **Macbeth, Act V, Sc. V**

A dear friend of mine, a natural witch of the old school, for years, would set up an ancestral altar every October/November to honor her loved ones who'd passed. I also had Daemonolater friends who did something similar though admittedly I didn't start the practice until I'd lost a few people close to me. The ancestral altar is not specific to Daemonolatry. Many cultures (Eastern and Western) have erected shrines and altars to the dead.

Perhaps one of the most famous of all festivals of the dead is *Día de los Muertos,* a holiday celebrated in Mexico on November 2 which follows the Catholic holiday of All Saints Day on November 1. On this day the ancestors who've passed are honored with elaborate altars decorated with sugar skulls and marigolds. Pictures of deceased relatives and personal items of the deceased may also be put on the altars. People will gather in cemeteries to pray and there may be parades, feasts, and other festivities. Similar celebrations happen in other cultures as well (including parts of Europe, Africa, and Asia).

In Daemonolatry it's much the same thing. The altar is a small table (or large depending on your preference) and often contains pictures of deceased loved ones, items from the deceased, letters to the deceased, prayer candles, sigils of gods or Daemons specific to death and the safety of the dead, and flowers. These things are not the only things you can put on your altar. What you do with your altar is up to you. Some people place skulls on the altar and they're almost always draped with a black altar cloth.

Daemonolatry High Priest Brad Morlan had this to say about ancestral altars. *"My grandfather always told us that when we place pictures on the altar, never include a picture of someone living... even if the main focus of the picture, is on someone who has died who is in the picture. According to him, this brings the death energy to the people who are still alive, and may wreak havoc in their lives."*

Some people ask about offerings to the dead and I suppose it would depend on your personal feelings about that. Some people don't give offerings at all, others will offer prayer candles, and others still prefer to use the traditional offerings related to the particular pantheon they work with (if they're wanting to research historical offerings). This is entirely up to the practitioner. It's been my experience there really are no wrong answers here. The Daemons will give you a hint if they want something specific and the dead require no offerings. The fact that you honor your ancestors is a beautiful thing done out of respect and reverence for those who came before.

It's super important at this juncture to point out that death is not always a time for sorrow and grief. It is also a time for celebration! In South America, throughout Mexico and through Native North American Indian tribes, the ancestors are celebrated and are said to help the living with protection and advice, even from beyond the grave. So death is both mourned and celebrated in these cultures. In Asia, there is a strong connection to the ancestors as well. They are honored in the same way and also sought to help the living. Such traditions, as I said earlier in this book, span the world over. So the important lesson we in the West can take from this is we can learn to celebrate those who came before us. Putting up a yearly ancestral altar can be a way bringing this celebration into our lives.

S. Connolly

Tools and Methods for

Necromancy and Necromantic Divination

A man's dying is more the survivors' affair than his own.
~Thomas Mann, The Magic Mountain

Again, I'd like to remind the reader that divination is only a tool. Do not use it to make every decision in your life or allow yourself to become addicted. Situations and futures change and most often divination only tells of what could be, not necessarily what is. Also, another gentle reminder, please approach this work with respect and reverence for the dead. They are more apt to cooperate.

A Tip (from B. Morlan's family traditions)
After any kind of channeling or divination, eat a piece of salt to help ground yourself. Rock salt, solar sea salt, and kosher salt are all acceptable.

Spirit Boards

You can't really discuss necromancy to any great length without at least touching on the use of spirit boards. In the book *The Daemonolater's Guide to Daemonic Magick* I discuss how to prepare a board for Daemonic interaction (only) and tell a story as to why this is important - I will repeat it here as it bears repeating.

With Ouija/Spirit Boards there is a very specific method of preparation that must be followed if you are going to get Daemonic entities ONLY to come through the board. Otherwise you open the board to anything that wishes to communicate with you and that can turn out really bad. I realize that most people reading this will be surprised to learn that even Daemon Worshipers have a deep respect for the proper use of the ouija/spirit board and that we'd warn the practitioner at all about them. I assure you this warning comes from personal experience. Boards (made by Parker Brothers or not) are NOT TOYS. As a matter of fact, I wish they'd quit selling the damn things at Toys R Us. All it takes is one board and a *real* medium – and the boards can become very dangerous. Sure – thousands of people use the boards with no ill effects at all. The key component is a medium. Once you put a medium on the board – every "thing" from the other side is going to see that portal open and whoever or whatever gets there first can attach itself to the board. Sometimes that "whatever" is very bad.

Let me share a story just to drive this point home. When I was a teenager I got my first ouija board and contacted my first otherworld entity who called itself Samuel. Samuel started out being very helpful but soon showed his true colors when a friend, we'll call her R, decided to talk back to the board. "Samuel, you're an idiot," she said. Next thing we knew, a set of invisible hands (that were clearly leaving marks even though nothing was there) were choking R and lifting her off of the ground. She began to turn blue. I yelled at the thing to stop and flipped the board upside down. R was released.

I put the board away and didn't touch it for several months. The next time we pulled it out I took it to my friend S's. When we pulled it out, same thing. We got Samuel. This time, he lied to us and was clearly being a problem. I left the board with S. Several days later she called me to tell me something was in her basement (it was a finished basement so it's not like it was scary to begin with). *It* was turning on and off lights late at night and opening and closing doors. *It* would also travel through the basement causing cold spots and call out her name when she was the only one home.

Whatever Samuel was, he had attached himself to the board and was using it as a portal (that I myself had inadvertently opened, being the medium I am) to gain entry into this world, manifesting a full out haunting.

After much research through books (we didn't have Internet back then) we discovered the best way to remove an unwanted "thing" attached to a Ouija board was to burn the board and planchette, collect the ashes, separate the ashes into two or three separate containers, and distribute those ashes into separate bodies of running water. So in one night, we did this, walking miles to the next river and then another mile to a creek (the only running water around).

This effectively removed Samuel from my friend's house and things went back to normal. No more cold spots, no more doors opening and shutting, no more disembodied voices, and no more lights turning on and off.

This is why it is of the utmost importance that for Daemonic Divination work (I said Daemonic) you use a new board that has never been used and **prepare it first**.

Board Preparation

This method of prepping a board will exclude everything but Daemons. You might just want to keep two separate boards.

(Doesn't matter if your board is Parker Brothers or not) You have to prep the planchette.

- Delepitore or Azlyn Oleum OR sage oil
- 1 candle, color of your choice.
- 1 small stone your choice (think - fits on head of pin)

S. Connolly

Generally this is done inside an elemental circle by witness of Satan (or your All), Delepitore (or equivalent), and/or Azlyn (or equivalent).

First you anoint the board and the planchette with the oil. Then, you drip candle wax on the planchette to cover it (NOT the indicator window). The sigil of a Daemon of your choice is carved into the wax or drawn on the planchette with oleum. The planchette is anointed again. The stone is affixed, with a tiny dab of glue, at the center of the indicator window (this is why it must be small). You can burn temple incense if you want.

If you do it right - nothing but Daemons will come through the board.

Mind you this will not necessarily make a board work for you. You either have mediumship ability with a board or you don't. This just ensures that nothing but Daemons come through a particular board. If you dedicate a board to your death Daemons, you can effectively use this board for necromancy.

Now for necromancy without the Daemonic you may not necessarily WANT a Daemonic board. However, you may want to use it within a prepared ritual space in attempt to filter out the riff raff.

Using The Board

One of the primary ingredients necessary to use a board correctly is you need someone who is a medium. That means – someone who is sensitive to otherworldly entities and with whom the entities can effectively communicate. Some people – by their mere presence – stilt the flow of energies making communication impossible. The medium(s) ONLY should place up to three fingers on the planchette. For lap boards or one medium, they may use both hands, two or three fingers on each hand. Yes, this means that ONE person can work a board by his/her-self. If the medium senses that anyone in the room is blocking him/her, she should ask that person to leave. A block feels like someone holding you back when you're trying to walk forward. You know that feeling? If you feel that – stop, find the block and remove it.

Ask for the Daemonic entity you would like to speak with and the planchette should start moving. I get figure eights, others get circles. Then you begin asking questions. Keep a pad of paper and pen ready (someone else to record the session is ideal). When you have made contact you will feel a feathery, electric sensation move through the top of your hands and through your fingers and you'll also feel a strange energy "pressure" even though your fingers are still resting lightly on the planchette. You may feel that electricity feeling up through your wrists (it almost tickles). It's not an unpleasant sensation, just strange at first.

The Daemonic force or entity responds to each question by moving the planchette from letter to letter to spell out words. More sensitive mediums may also find they get images and/ or actually "hear" in their mind's eye the words before they're finished being spelt out. And when they think the words, the planchette will jump to yes. If you are this type of medium your sessions will be much more productive. Expect that your medium (or you if you're the medium) will be tired after long durations of board work.

Prepping a board in such a way can keep all but Divine Intelligence from coming through. I have strong feelings about board usage and discourage anyone who isn't a trained and experienced medium from using them. Inexperienced people who use boards can potentially open portals causing anything from the other side to get through. More often than not this will produce hauntings or poltergeist activity in the home where the board was used. If this happens - do NOT throw the board away. DO NOT! Instead, safely burn the board and planchette (an outdoor fire pit is ideal), separate the ashes into two or three parts and distribute each part into a separate body of running water. This will often close the portal and remove whatever is in the house or space. Now - if that doesn't work, you may need to perform a portal closing, banishing, or "sending off" depending on the type of spirit you've unleashed. Now you see why an experienced medium is important. You need to know the difference between an "Other" and a human spirit and a Daemon. They're all different types of entities.

This is why this next section is NOT for beginners and inexperienced mediums. Boards have the potential to be dangerous. On that same token, they can be useful tools. Here's the thing - you want to speak with the dead in the most direct form possible. For many mediums their natural gifts of clairsentience, clairvoyance, or clairaudience leaves a lot to be desired in the "direct" department. Spirit boards, also known as Ouija boards, are one of the tools that can help with direct communication. The difficulty arises because boards open indiscriminate portals to the other side. *Indiscriminate* is the keyword here. Indiscriminate can be unpredictable and dangerous and can allow everything through from Daemons to grounded human spirits, to *others*. It's usually the *others* that can turn out to be nasty. Though sometimes you'll get a malevolent grounded human spirit, too.

There are several ways in which use of a spirit board can be handled. First - knowing the difference between human, helpful, and harmful spirits is essential.

You can use a board without prep (be very careful).

You can use a prepped board and ask the Daemonic to bring through the appropriate spirit to talk to you - this is a very precise method that seems to work well. But you'll want to adjust your preparation to dedicate the board specifically to one of the death Daemons (as described above). A necromantic board should ONLY be used for necromancy. Whereas a general Daemonic communication board will be used for all Daemonic communication. Yes, this does mean having different boards for different situations.

The board helps with communication by allowing the medium to channel the spirit (usually limited to the hands) so the spirit can move the planchette to make words. The Clairsentient may immediately get the words in their head after the first few letters. The Clairvoyant may see the spirit speaking and the Clairaudient may actually "hear" the words in their mind. So this tool merely helps the words form in this sense.

The ideal method for this is to have the medium work the board while another person records the session in a notebook. Having more than one person's hand on the planchette is more likely to stifle the communication rather than encourage it unless you have two mediums and both can work effectively together. There are a lot of factors that weigh into this so it's often just easier to keep it simple. Let one person record while another person works the board. If the medium feels any blocks, one by one people should be removed from the room to find the person blocking the session. Some folks are just natural deterrents to effective communication with the other side.

Skrying and Necromancy

Skrying Mirrors/Crystals and Bowls

Skrying as a method of communication and divination is best left to those who are clairvoyant (or those whose medium abilities allow them to see images). One of the more terrifying experiences of my youth as an untrained and ignorant necromancer was an incident with a skrying mirror. For over fifteen years I wasn't able to use a skrying mirror for fear the dead, decaying thing that I once saw in the mirror would still be there, smirking at me. Of course I've gotten over that hurdle, but it was one hell of a hurdle to cross.

First, don't use skrying as a parlor game, especially when dealing with the dead or the death Daemons. If you want to scare the crap out of yourself – this is the easiest way to do it.

Basically skrying is a form of divination in which you peer into a reflective surface and visually see images. In necromancy you can use this method to see and speak with the dead. The three most common forms of skrying are Mirror Skrying, Crystal Skrying, and Bowl Skrying.

To prepare your skrying equipment you can anoint the devices directly with oleums of Death Daemons. For skrying mirrors, you can put the sigils of Death Daemons on the frame. For crystals, you should probably leave them intact and untouched. For Bowls, you can paint sigils directly onto the outside of the bowls. As with most divination sessions you probably ought to consider working within a balanced, Daemonically charged circle (with Death Daemons obviously) for both balance and to keep unwanted influences away while you work. While

S. Connolly

it's not a foolproof method, it is a little safer than working without any safety at all.

Creating the Mirror:

You can buy a skrying mirror. They're basically mirrors with a black backing. Or, if you have some time and ambition, you can create your own mirror.

The first step is to buy a picture frame with glass intact (or a piece of glass that will fit into a frame). Do not buy plastic! Make sure it's real glass and the thicker the glass, the better because it gives more depth. Choose a frame that has some aesthetic appeal for you (i.e. something you really like). You can get frames at dollar stores and thrift stores inexpensively.

Remove the glass from the frame and clean it completely (same process for a mirror). With some glossy black oil based enamel paint, paint one side of the glass (or the back silver side of the mirror). You will need to apply as many coats as necessary to make sure no light passes through. Allow the paint to dry completely between coats.

Paint any sigils or symbols you wish on your frame. Finally, put the glass (or mirror) back into the frame, the paint side of the glass on the inside. Make sure you have some cardboard or felt board against the painted side to keep the glass from getting scuffed. Use a collector plate stand to prop your skrying mirror up (or if you're using a frame that came with a stand, that can work too) and you're done. You can get collector plate stands at hobby and craft stores and usually large discount stores like Walmart or Target.

Finally – you can use a regular mirror. However, many people won't get results with a regular mirror unless they're very sensitive. You can try it and if it works for you, great. But if it doesn't work, try a black mirror.

Crystals:

There are numerous crystals you can use for gazing. Some are cut in the shape of pyramids or other geometrics. The most popular are crystal gazing balls. Glass can be used in place of crystal, but some believe that crystal itself allegedly lends better to gazing/skrying. Regardless, the ball should be kept clean and free of fingerprints and dust.

Skrying Bowls:

Your average skrying bowl is dark in color (either black or some other dark color) and you put water, ink, oil or blood into the bowl for skrying to create the reflective surface. Skrying fluids used in the bowl should be of even color. So mix liquids beforehand, for example if you're diluting blood in water, or ink in water, or using blood or ink in oil. Some liquids separate. In some methods of skrying this is desirable. In others, it's not. Depending on whether you're reading the shapes in the water (as with tea leaf reading) then you might use oil in a water based fluid, or vice versa. If you're not doing that kind of "reading" or skrying – a fluid, solid color with no separation is best. Inks, blood, and waters often work well together. Oil is one of those substances you should use alone for standard skrying.

How to Scry

Start your ritual by invoking the Daemons of Death you are working with. Then, within a prepared ritual space, flank your skrying device with candles, then gaze into your skrying device and clear your mind. Completely let go and allow the images to come. Usually the reflective surface will fade to black (or seem hazy or smoky) and then the images will come forth. Sometimes they're clear, sometimes not. Try your best not to give a voice to the images, let them come and go. Just remember them. When you pause, write down what you've seen or say aloud what you see (having a recorder there, human or electronic is handy), giving your mind time to process the images. If we try too soon to process and define the images, we can end up stilting the flow of the images and holding ourselves back from stronger images.

For some people, skrying is not easy because the images are far too disturbing or unsettling for them to handle. Others won't get images at all because they have no gifts for clairvoyance. The only way to know if skrying works for you is to try it. If it doesn't, there are plenty of other divination devices and methods to try and learn. If the images are weak – you can continue to practice and hone your skill as eventually they'll become stronger.

Automatic Writing

Automatic writing in a favorite of many mediums/necromancers and can be a useful tool when working necromancy. There are varying opinions on Daemonic ritual space constructs when performing automatic writing. I'm of the opinion that you have to do what works best for you as the medium. Some mediums like the safety and comfort zone of the Daemonic ritual space (created with Death Daemons of course) while others prefer to work without the Daemonic, not wanting or needing the Daemonic for such things. Automatic writing itself is yet another form of channeling wherein the medium opens him/herself up to the dead, allowing the dead use of the medium's hands to write out responses to questions. Always while working certain necromancies having an assistant can be helpful. Not necessary most certainly, but helpful at times. Especially in cases of recording sessions or during automatic writing. Oftentimes automatic writing is erratic. Pencil and loose sheets of paper work best because the medium can change paper immediately and pencil ensures you're not going to accidently write all over yourself or furniture with something permanent. I know that sounds like a strange thing to bring up, but trust me, one too many of my blouses was messed up with permanent black marker back when I did a great deal of automatic writing with marker. I finally started using pencil because of that.

Pendulums

Some mediums have had luck working with pendulums during necromantic work. As usual, you would establish which swings are yes vs. no using baseline questions, then call upon the dead, and then proceed to ask questions and record the answers. Again, whether you do such work in a Daemonic prepared ritual space is up to you. Some necromancers find the Daemonic energy amplifies the work, others find it hinders it. Again, you must find the right balance for you. Many of my necromancer friends will carve or paint a sigil of one of the death Daemons on the pendulum stone. Some good choices for stones for necromancy - Azurite (helps initiate contact with spirits), Quartz (amplifies psychic abilities), Shaman Stones (good for initiating contact), Tanzinite (good for initiating contact), Blue Tigers Eye (opens conduits for easier communication with spirits) or any tiger eye for that matter, but most people I talked to preferred Blue Quartz and Blue Tigers Eye. Both quite popular choices among the necromancers I've surveyed.

Contacting Specific Spirits

During your career as a necromancer it's only natural that people are going to come to you asking you contact particular spirits of deceased loved ones. It is important that the necromancer have something to work with. Some necromancers can get away with just knowing a name. Others need a picture, and others still need a personal item from the deceased. Attuning yourself to the energy of an item once belonging to the deceased is probably the easiest way to make contact. To do this, hold the item in your hand and concentrate on it. Feel the vibration of it. Attune yourself to the vibration (some people need to chant or meditate on it for some time) and then pull that vibration from the other side of the veil to you (in your mind, of course).

A strong medium can do this with pictures and very experienced mediums can do this with just a name. Some don't need a name at all, but can actually pull the information and connection directly from the person they're reading for. I am admittedly not of the latter type. I prefer objects from the deceased along with names and pictures for the most accurate contact possible. You may find your own combination that works for you. Not all mediums are created equally and we all have different strengths, weaknesses, energies and vibrations of our own that effect how our abilities work and can be used. The key here is to experiment and find out what works best for your abilities.

High Priest Morlan offered the following family ritual to contact a specific spirit of the dead.

A Necromantic Rite
Courtesy B. Morlan

Set up a triangle in the middle of the ritual space using 3 candles. The color of these candles will depend on the deceased and their sun sign. For example: If they were an air element, you'd use blue or white etc. If the sun-sign of the deceased is unknown use black candles. In the center of this triangle of candles place the person's name on a piece of parchment. Then each person in the session should add a few drops of blood to the parchment and also at each candle.

Invoke Leviathan *"Jedan tasa hoet naca Leviathan"* asking for the emotional stability and strength to come through to connect with the dead.

After invoking Leviathan, say the name of the person 3 times, while thinking of the connection to your own blood and the essence of the loved one. This will produce the desired contact with the specific spirit. When the session is finished, burn the paper in the offering bowl. Thank Leviathan and close the ritual. Take the ashes from the burnt paper and disperse into running water.

Channeling

Channeling Daemons is one thing. Channeling the spirits of the dead is another. This process is extremely helpful if you want to allow the deceased to use your body to speak to their loved ones directly, or can be used to supplement an automatic writing session.

Channeling is basically a process wherein you allow a spirit to take over your body so that it can perform physical action, or more often, can use your mouth to speak directly to others in the room.

Oftentimes, I don't recommend channeling unless you are working with several people. Sometimes, the person channeling can get lost in the feeling of having their mind disconnected from their body, and won't remember what was said. Other times, the person channeling could panic (if it's their first time) and it's useful to have someone else there to help bring them back from the experience.

In this section I'll explain some merging techniques and controlled channeling techniques that will help you channel. If during the exercises you do go into channeling, don't panic. Spirits take a great deal of energy to manifest and they generally don't have the power to possess you for long periods of time. Now if you want to learn about channeling the Daemonic, I suggest *The Daemonolater's Guide to Daemonic Magick* because channeling a Daemon is a whole different experience than channeling a human spirit.

Why Channel?

Channeling can be useful during group divination and I've personally used channeling (with a Daemonic entity) in paranormal investigations as a way to identify what is happening in a house or location. So knowing how to perform both Daemonic channeling and channeling of human spirits are both equally useful to the practicing necromancer.

How does one channel?

There are three basic steps to channeling. The invitation, the merging, and finally allowing the entity to enter the body. The last part is the hardest for most people because it's instinctive for us to want to maintain control of our bodies. For others, this is going to come quite naturally.

A Note of Warning: When I say channeling is not dangerous, I mean, it's not dangerous for mentally stable individuals who are working within a well prepared and balanced ritual space. This means you have invoked Daemonic entities (in this case, of Death) into the space so that the spirits you're actually working with are the only ones who can slip into your body and so you won't be overtaken by an "Other". Not all spirits or entities are harmless.

A Channeling Meditation:

Meditate on the person you're trying to contact using a picture or item imbued with their essence. Allow their energy to surround you. Surrender to it. Merge with it. Remember your breath. Relax. Allow all emotions, feelings, thoughts to flow freely. Their thoughts become your thoughts and vice versa. You are intertwined with this spirit.

To Channel, you simply let go and allow the Daemon to take over when you feel that you and the Daemon's energies are merged sufficiently.

What to Expect:

Many people describe the feeling of hearing someone talking with their voice, but it not being them. They often report feeling disconnected from their own mind and body and surrounded in blackness. I have had this same experience. The second you feel panicked or like you want to return into your mind to regain control, you just shove the spirit out of the way and re-enter.

More importantly you should know the people involved can get really freaked out by a spirit being channeled. It's important you discuss with the participants what they should expect so that no one is caught off guard or panics during a session. The others present should expect the medium's voice and personality to completely change. (S)he might use words or phrases (s)he would never use, her face may contort and take on a different appearance, her voice may sound gruff or even plural, and in some instances those present may experience paranormal phenomena during the session including actually seeing physically manifested entities separate or merge with the

S. Connolly

host medium's, stray lights and shadows, sounds, and even objects moving. I have experienced all of these phenomena at least once during a channeling session, so expect it.

To leave the state of Channeling at will, simply tell the Spirit (obviously in your mind) that you would like to return to your body now and if you have problems, just give them a good mental shove. You should find yourself back in your body and in full control of your faculties. You may also feel like you're waking up from a nap. Channeling can be a very draining experience. Some mediums may choose to do energy raising rituals before and after channeling sessions in order to increase their own personal energy.

*Please note I say give spirits a mental shove and in the very beginning of the book I warn you to be respectful. Sometimes angry or confused spirits need a firm hand. Don't be deliberately disrespectful because you could get yourself in trouble. Instead, be firm and resolved and don't allow the spirit to push you around. But at the same time, it is possible to still show a great deal of respect.

Helping Grounded Spirits Cross Over

Death is a delightful hiding place for weary men.

~Herodotus

One of the many reasons a necromancer might be called into a situation is to help the spirits of the deceased cross over. Sometimes human or animal spirits find themselves grounded. When this is the case it is up to the necromancer to communicate with the spirit, point out the light, and help them cross over. Sometimes this can be done with simple communication as described in the communication and channeling sections of this book. Other times, however, a spirit must be crossed forcibly. This may sometimes be the case of severe hauntings or poltergeist activity involving angry or stubborn spirits. In this case there is a Daemonolatry necromantic ritual that can be used to forcibly remove the spirit from its grounded state and cross it over. To do this you will need nerves of steel.

S. Connolly

First, a story because stories are wonderful ways to illustrate why you might want a ritual like this. Back in the early 90's a roommate and I were living in a house built in the early 1900's. It was one of the servant/farm hand houses on the property of what was once part of a large farm. At that time I was still very inexperienced, so was surprised to discover that after a few months living in the house and working magick there - I'd stirred up the grounded spirits still on the property, including one in the house. It started that items would move when my roommate and I were at work. We'd come home to find all the cupboards in the kitchen open. Then we started hearing the noises at night and doors would open and close on their own. We'd also hear a lot of noise from the bathroom including running water and splashing when no one was in there and no water was running. Finally, one day I was in the bathroom and my roommate was in the kitchen right off the bathroom and I mentioned that I was getting tired of the "ghost" because it was keeping me up. At that point, a hairbrush lifted off the dressing table in the bathroom and was hurled across the room at my head from three feet away. Luckily the brush didn't strike me. It hit the door right next to my head.

At that point I decided to perform an exorcism. I got together with my teacher and high priestess, got the ritual, and performed it. The initial exorcism didn't work. Instead, it caused the paranormal activity to increase. The day after the exorcism my roommate and I returned home to find all the items used in the exorcism toppled over and on the floor, all the cupboard doors were open, and broken dishes were all over the kitchen. It was at that point my roommate and I decided to call in a real necromancer to take care of the problem and it was the first time I watched someone far more experienced than I cross a grounded spirit over.

Once the rite began and the Daemons were invoked, I noticed that the temperature drop and the energy of the room changed. The temperature dropped about ten degrees and the air in the room seemed "charged". The hair on my arms actually stood on end. Eurynomous was invoked and asked to literally remove the disruptive spirit from my home and to send it to the other side. The Daemon literally "escorted" the spirit off the property and beyond the veil. It was one of the most powerful rites I've ever witnessed. All paranormal activity in the house and the grounds immediately ceased after that. See the rituals in the Necromantic Ritual Section of the book to find a rite of this nature.

The Abbot from the Dance of Death
By Hans Holbein

Working With Daemons and The Dead

I get asked this question a great deal. "How do I summon a Daemon to help me speak with a deceased loved one?"

Are you a natural medium? If so, work with any of the Death Daemons. If you perform a basic ritual in their honor and give an offering, then, within the prepared ritual space, use your device or method of choice (a lot of Necromancers also work with mirrors or astrally), you should very easily be able to speak with the deceased. This does seem to be easier to do for those whose medium abilities aren't as developed around the end of October and early November when the veil is the thinnest. For those who are developed mediums your success will depend on your skill level, your overall health and frame of mind, and the background vibration. A gate opening may be required.

See the ritual section of the book for more information about this.

If you're not a natural medium I would suggest seeking out a Necromancer and asking them to perform the task for you. Getting beyond the veil and bringing forth the right deceased human spirit and imparting the information can be tricky business for those who don't have a natural affinity for necromancy. It's a bit more complicated than just "doing a spell or a ritual" and poof - you can suddenly speak to the deceased.

Death really is just another state of existence and to be honest, once a spirit crosses the veil to the other side I personally don't think they should be asked to come back unless there is a dire circumstance or their death is very recent and the living still haven't had closure. Usually when that happens though, spirits will stick around until they're sure their loved ones are okay. My deceased grandmother took two weeks after her death before visiting me and making what I thought was her final contact. Yet almost a month later I was given a dream insisting I visit her grave. Evidently she still wasn't ready to go.

Once again, the general rule about necromancy (i.e. raising the dead) is don't do it unless you absolutely have to and you know what you're doing.

Now let's discuss the composition of the Daemonolatry ritual space ala Necromancy style. I like to choose four Death Daemons (for me it's usually Eurynomous, Anubis, Bune, and Babael – and since I'm not a hard polytheist and I view the Daemonic archetypically I can work across hierarchies like this without any fear that the world will end) and invoke one from each quarter of the ritual circle. Elemental alignment isn't necessarily important but you can choose to construct the circle this way. Personally I work my circle with Eurynomous to the North, Babael East, Bune South and Anubis West. Why? I am viewing them as the cycle of life. Babael is the birth and the child, Bune is the teenager and father, Anubis is the elder and Eurynomous represents the final Death. Go around the circle again and the cycle repeats. There is also the consideration that Babael is the first realization of Death, Bune is the first realization of mortality, Anubis is the acceptance of death, and Eurynomous is the passing. It's just something that works for me.

To perform the ritual space construction you approach each point at which you've placed the Daemonic sigil and you invoke the Daemonic Divine by employing the ZD sigil and their enns either through vibration or chanting. I prefer vibration. There's an atmospheric changing quality about the vibration of enns that appeals to me and my own personal energy signatures.

Now instead of tracing the ZD sigil in the air, I do this on the ground over the sigil. Instead of a ritual dagger I prefer to use an oak wand with a clear quartz crystal at the end of it. A stave will work in a pinch provided it also is made of oak and has a quartz crystal in it. I use such devices as they help me to focus the intent and energy into the invocation and I've found the concentration facilitates stronger and faster gate opening. For further information on ritual constructs and invocation see either *The Complete Book of Demonolatry* or *The Daemonolater's Guide to Daemonic Magick* (which talks more about ritual construct). Performing such invocations outdoors is more powerful. And yes, you can perform it in a graveyard if you insist, but it's not necessary. Then I move onto the gate opening and using the gate opening vibrations I've learned,

I'll open each gate which essentially floods the area with the Daemonic energy. The portal opens and the session can begin. (See rituals later in this book for gate opening.)

Below you'll find the ZD invocation symbol. Start at the arrow, stop at the dot. To learn more about basic Daemonolatry invocation see *The Complete Book of Demonolatry, The Daemonolater's Guide to Daemonic Magick, or Demonolatry Rites.*

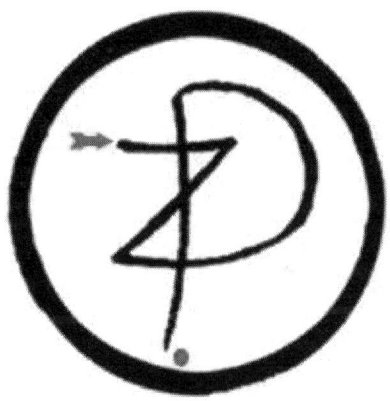

S. Connolly

Preparing for Death

We understand death for the first time when he puts his hand upon one whom we love.

~Madame de Stael

As human beings we are all slated for death – eventually. So it's only prudent to discuss death in the most practical manner possible befitting a magus who uses any common sense in his approach to magick and consequently necromancy.

There are essential things we all must consider when our time comes. Certainly some will say, "Hell with it, let my family or the State deal with my corpse." And this section isn't for you. But for those of you who wish your final wishes to be taken seriously please continue to look over this chapter for the sake of preparing yourself for death.

First, there is the matter of funeral arrangements. I find it prudent to encourage friends and family to write out what their wishes are. If you want a pagan funeral ceremony and your family wants a Catholic one, you may want to make your wishes known in your will. Of course you also have to remember that funerals are for the living, not the dead. You may have wanted a pagan funeral, but a Catholic funeral may make your family feel better. These are the types of things one must consider when preparing for his own eventual demise. Other serious considerations include burial vs. cremation. Will you buy your headstone and plot now so when the time comes your family won't have the unexpected expense? Should you get life insurance to make sure you don't leave your family with the expense? Even a cheap, no frills funeral can cost thousands.

There are also a few documents you'll want to look into regardless your age.

- Wills
- Living Wills
- DNR Orders
- Organ Donation

Yes, it's a lot. And why have I included it in this book? For some reason Eurynomous felt it was important that I at least touch on these subjects otherwise I probably wouldn't have. A book discussing necromancy should include a frank discussion of death, shouldn't it? Besides, leaving nothing behind puts you at risk for the State or a family member (one you may not like a whole lot) being put in charge of distributing or getting rid of your assets.

Don't have any assets? Well then that probably won't apply to you. However, DNR Orders, Organ Donation, and Living Wills are very important documents and everyone over the age of twenty-one (possibly even eighteen) should have them in order. None of us is guaranteed another day, after all.

Prayers for the Dead

Death is a debt we all must pay.

~Euripides

S. Connolly

The Final Farewell

Oh dearly departed in death we do seek thee.
By Eurynomous you pass from this world to the next.
I pray for you dearly and now you must leave me
Till we meet again with my labored last breath.

To Protect The Dearly Departed

Bune shall take you through the veil.
And Babael keep your memory sacred.
With Him you will cross the river now
And shall you never be re-awakened.

For A Beloved Pet

May the light of All bless and keep you.
May the Daemonic Divine lead you there.
Back to all that is, with my love.
My beloved pet. Amen.

Another for Pets

Even though this mere creature of Belial was not a man nor woman, (s)he was my friend and companion in life. Now, our Lord Eurynomous has taken her soul in peaceful rest. Thus we lay her to the ground, to the earth from whence she came. In sorrow we release her and in joy do we celebrate the dawn of her passing. Blessed are the beasts for their love in unconditional. Blessed are the beasts for their judgment lies in truth. Protect and keep her, so be it.

For a Child

Lord Baalberith, please watch over this little child. (S)he has come to you in death. As protector of souls, comfort and guide her to her resting place. May Babael guard her that no harm shall befall her. A life so young forsaken. We weep and find comfort in knowing she is now, and ever shall be among kindred. As her energy was in life so it returns to its source. Blessed are the children for their innocence. Blessed is this child. Lord Eurynomous protect and keep her, so be it.

A Funeral Oration

In darkness there comes a ray of light in the promise of rebirth foretold by our dark Lords. Hail Eurynomous and Baalberith. May Babael keep this burial place sacred and un-soiled. We pray you Lord Eurynomous, for our loved one's safe passage to Unsere who brings life from the desolate.

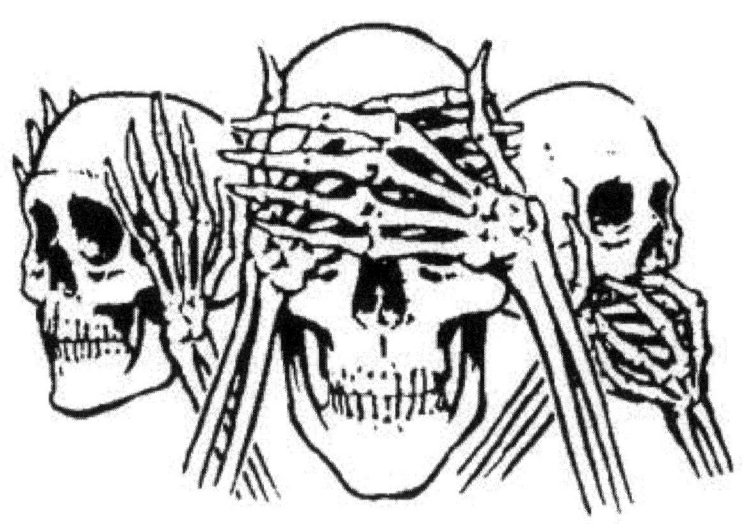

Necromantic
Rituals

Funerary Rite

The following ritual has been shared courtesy the OFS and is from their official Ritus Sacerdotal text, which is the standard text for priests.

The funeral setting provides a challenge for the Priest. The entire experience is an opportunity to communicate the warmth of a loving Satan (Eurynomous, Baalberith, Babaal) at a time of grief and pain. Preparation is a necessity. The conducting of a funeral is the most solemn of occasions and it requires the sincere attentions of the Priest to the grieving family members. If the Priest knows the family, it would be appropriate for the Priest to talk with family members to ask each one if there is anything special that they would like said. Usually one family member or friend assumes the responsibility for the planning for the ceremony and services.

When death comes, the Priest becomes a central figure in bringing comfort and hope to the sorrowing. The examples here are for funeral chapel and graveside ceremonies.

Emphasis should be upon the need to set minds upon the eternal truths of the Daemonic Divine rather than the mortal remains of the person. A brief message or a lesson from Group Scripture as part of the service will help to fulfill this need. Choose something of significance to the loved ones.

Those who perform funerary rites should conduct themselves professionally and proudly as a representative of the Daemonic, the culture and the community of believers according to the Faith. Not all funerals are religious in nature and the Necromantic Priest should be prepared to offer a civil ceremony without references to Satan or any particular belief system. The decision of the family, Demonolators or not, must be honored as this is a one-time event and the memory that remains must prevail positively in the Priest's benefit.

The first aspect that arises in the funeral experience is the availability of the Priest to the family for pastoral care and the ceremony itself. Death does not occur on a schedule. Those necromancers who offer their services to a community must be available at a moment's notice.

This adds to the importance of the Priest planning well and being prepared to call into being the presence of Satan to comfort the family and friends. Depending upon how "religious" the family wishes the ceremony to be, the Priest should be prepared to deliver a message of Satan's love and hope or to equally well deliver a message of understanding and hope for those families not wishing to have a religious-oriented service.

Some families may wish to have a civil type ceremony where the religious aspects are not dwelt upon. In these types of ceremonies the aspects of comforting, love, concern, well-being of the surviving family members and friends are to be taken note of. It is appropriate for civil ceremonies to focus upon the lifetime achievements and community involvement of the deceased. Simply removing the words Satan, Lucifer, any Daemonic Names and Amen may be sufficient to the family to be absent from a religious tone. Still the focus of the ceremony is to provide comfort and a caring attitude to the family and friends attending. A Priest may be called upon for a Committal ceremony at the graveside for the purposes of the customs and tradition of the culture. Oftentimes there is a component of a military salute to the deceased.

Even families that are not grouped, oftentimes they become warmly disposed to religion at special events in life; birth, baptism, marriage and death. An aspect of the "oneness" or of the "eternal" essence is felt at these particular times in life and Satan is called upon for guidance, strength, understanding and comfort. If a family is not grouped and wishes a civil or humanistic service, it is the responsibility of the Priest to provide that type of ceremony with aspects of religion left out. Remember always that funerals are for the living not for the deceased and that **the needs of the bereaved are utmost.**

The Priest is important to the ceremony and to the

cultural aspects of how we care for our deceased. In addition, the Priest is important as being a comforting soul to the family and friends. The Priest presides over the ceremony and is directly responsible for the well programmed and carried out ceremony.

Oftentimes it is requested that either a family member or close friend to give a EULOGY, which is a short talk of remembrance of the individual. There is no question of "appropriate or inappropriate" because the ceremony is for the living and anything that is requested by the family should be accommodated by the Priest. A eulogy does not have to be solemn and can contain gentle humor that assists in the remembrance of the individual.

Not so strangely it does seem odd for a Demonolatry funeral rite to take place in a crematorium/funeral home chapel (even though this has been known to occasionally happen) so most rites are done at a family home after the cremation or at the gravesite.

I was asked by one of my beta readers if the funerary rite serves to help the dead sever ties with the living so they can pass on. My answer to this is, not really. For the most part, most spirits don't have any problems passing or crossing over. Some spirits may stick around to see their loved ones off in their own way. This ritual really serves the purpose of comforting the living. Now some will tell you that the farewells, once burnt, will be taken to the afterlife with the deceased, but it's my personal belief (based on what I've been told by the spirits themselves) that spirits can see things clearer from where they are and they know how their loved ones feel and what they think. It's amazing how things look from that side of the fence.

Feel free to modify the following rite to reflect your personal pantheon or the pantheon of the deceased.

The circle is constructed as always (for necromantic priests this will include all the Death Daemons being worked with). Selected items of the deceased are taken to the altar along with the urn. Eurynomous, Baalberith, and Babael are invited to preside during the rite. In a large bowl the deceased's items are placed. Each of the family members and friends write their farewells prior to the rite and bring them with them to burn during the ceremony. Traditionally, most of the rite is done in silence to allow the mourners to reflect and mourn.

Each note/farewell is taken and burnt to ash and poured over the items, which will be buried or entombed with the ashes of the deceased. As each piece of paper is burnt the priest(ess) says: **"By Flereous your spirit is lifted. Sanctified in the sacred flames you shall rise."**

The incense is lit and waved over the altar. **"By Lucifer your spirit settles softly to return to Belial."**

Sand is poured into the bowl until everything is covered. **"By Belial you become one with him. His ground, now desolate and seemingly barren, shall rebirth you."**

Over that a chalice of consecrated water is poured. **"By Leviathan your spirit is rebirthed in the elements."**

The sigil of the Patron/Matron Demon is traced with the ritual dagger over the bowl. **"May [patron/matron name] guide you and keep you."**

"In the name of our Lord Satan it is done. We bid you farewell our brother/sister [name]."

Eulogies are done at this time if needed. The Priest(ess), assistants, and family members all take the urn and the bowl to the cemetery or burial place and entomb or bury the urn with the contents of the bowl and seal it. The outside of the tomb is anointed with the appropriate oleums and sigils.

Note that the Daemonic names used above CAN be changed to reflect your personal pantheon.

Appropriate Prayers for Funerals

Father Satan, we come today as people whose lives have been abruptly changed by the death of one whom we deeply love. This change has brought confusion, anger, loneliness, fear, and doubt. In the midst of these varied emotions, we long for peace and for endurance. We want to feel Your presence. Eurynomous, may the memories of precious moments shared sustain us in this time of grief. May those times of laughter and crying, joy and sorrow, energy and fatigue, conflict and peace, which mark our history with this beloved individual be the foundation of hope which sends us into tomorrow.

Our Daemonic Father, at a time when we are acutely aware of the death of a loved one, we thank You for Your living presence with us. Your unfailing companionship with us gives us comfort for today and courage for tomorrow.

Now may Satan, of hope, fill you with all joy and peace in believing, that you may abound in hope by the power of the The Ether of All that Is.

Parting the Veil

There are several methods for parting the veil. The first is relatively generic and is similar to any gate or portal opening ritual. After all, you're simply opening a gateway to another realm. It's the same concept.

For necromancy, parting the veil is a way of getting more direct contact. Open portals to the realm you're working with can funnel massive amounts of energy into a ritual working. Which in turn makes it easier to communicate with the spirits of the dead.

Regardless your purpose for opening a portal, whether necromantic or other, you must always be sure to close the portal once you've finished with it. Never leave a gaping hole leading to another world because you will open your ritual space to anything passing through. I've known people who opened portals, never closed them and who were later sorry they did because they weren't able to later close them. These people experienced severe and terrifying supernatural phenomena. See closing for more information.

To Part the Veil

Invoke the Daemonic Death Daemons you're working with via their Enns, above and below, then conjure the image of the shadowed plane. Imagine the barrier between worlds thinning out. Make sure you are forcing your energy toward this task and NOT internalizing it, or you could end up accidentally opening yourself up to possession (non-Daemonic), imbalance, and illness. Using the ritual blade, gently slice through the veil between this world and the next. Imagine the portal opening. At this point you should be able to *feel* the open portal. It will be cool and cause the air to move slightly as if a soft breeze is present. You may even experience a cold burst of air or a quick wind. Some may even be able to *see* the portal.

The Second Method

Do the above but when approaching each quadrant of the ritual space place your forearms together. Vibrate

"On na Ca" or *"An At"*

...While pulling your forearms apart as if opening a door. The action and the vibration further thins the veil. If you want a very thin veil, for twenty-four hours continue to do the parting ritual every two to four hours. The duration work continues to thin the veil in such a way that you may even get physical manifestation in the forms of shadows/shades or apparitions.

To close the portal when finished, follow the instructions that come next.

Closing the Veil

Closing the veil is a very similar process to closing an astral portal. After all, you're essentially doing the almost exact same thing. You're sealing a portal from this realm to the next. Most people may not realize that sometimes supernatural activity is a direct result of a left open portal to the other side. Some people actually open portals without realizing they do it. So the first step to closing a portal is for the necromancer to learn to identify one that's open. Do not use this ritual lightly. It is very strong and is meant to close giant, gaping holes that lead from the physical realm to the realm of the dead. The reason you'd want to close a portal is usually because of the metaphysical havoc including hauntings and poltergeist activity that open portals often encourage.

Signs of Open Portal Activity:

- A place where more than one entity or spirit dwells.
- Poltergeist activity
- Inanimate objects moving on their own.
- Disembodied voices
- Physical harassment of physical beings by otherworldly ones.
- Feelings of severe dread (check for high EMF and bad wiring first) or panic
- All of this centered around a single location (i.e. one spot).

- You will actually be able to feel the swirling energy of an open portal. It will push against you from up to ten feet from the actual opening epicenter.

Sure, this could also be a standard haunting. However, you'll know if it is just a haunting if the closing ritual doesn't work. In which case you might move onto a full out banishing or space cleansing ritual. A Daemonic exorcism (not to exorcise Daemons, but rather human and "other" spirits) **as a last resort**. For all intents and purposes, this ritual should be performed by gate keepers (preferred), walkers (second choice) or lastly - adepts. Gate keepers are actually people who live their entire lives in the presence of portals and understand their contents quite intimately. They are actually attracted to portals and will find themselves in the presence of one most their lives. Walkers (people who live between worlds) are people who can exist in a portal environment comfortably and are equally comfortable in both the astral and the physical realms. Finally, the adept being someone who can tell a portal from your standard haunting and can work successful magick to close it. Beginners and intermediate magicians can perform this ritual, it just may not properly work if you are not adept with energy work. Necromancers can fall into any of these categories.

This ritual works in three parts. First - you banish everything back into the portal via fumigation. Don't worry - Demons do not use the same portals as the dead to enter this world so you will not offend them. Second you'll be closing the portal and sealing it via energy fusing, and

S. Connolly

finally, you'll perform a second fumigation to make sure you remove everything from the space.

So first you'll want to make the initial fumigation incense. The fumigation incense consists of a simple blend of equal parts of white sandalwood and frankincense (crushed if possible). You will need one of those incense burners on a chain so you can swing it around. Swinging the incense clockwise, fumigate the entire area surrounding the portal paying special attention to areas with heavy activity (this may be a specific room in a house if that's where the portal is). While doing this, recite the incantation (with FORCE and conviction!) for sending all things back into the portal:

"In the name of Eurynomous [or your preferred Daemonic Force of Death] I send you back from whence you came! You are not welcome here! Leave us in peace!"

You may also vibrate the Enns of the Death Demons you're working with. This demonic energy will naturally deter and abolish the energy of lesser spirits.

Now - don't stop here or you could end up with more problems. Sometimes this ritual pisses off the angry spirits who were used to coming and going through an open portal. You may experience, at first, increased activity (especially if the rest of the ritual is not performed properly or the person performing it doesn't have the necessary "ability" to close the portal). You may have to re-do the entire ritual a second time. Don't be surprised if everything you used in the ritual turns up missing or is scattered around the house as if it was thrown in anger. If this happens - lather, rinse, repeat.

Now comes the part where the astral portal is fused. The person performing the fusing should, in the very least, be able to feel the portal. Someone who can actually 'see' the portal is even better (and your results are more apt to be successful). If you must, you can travel to the astral to perform this part of the ritual. In your mind's eye, see the portal opening. Using your own energy, encompass the portal and begin squeezing it shut, matching end to end. Once you bring all the edges together, use your own energy (you may invoke Daemonic force in Lucifuge Rofocal or Amducius using their Enns in order to draw from an outside energy source) to fuse the ends together, thus shutting the portal. As a final fusing, I like to add a "patch" over the opening in the form of a brilliant purple light that covers where the opening once was.

Séance

Communicate with Spirits

Workings of Necromancy can be, by far, some of the most dangerous workings out there because some spirits (notice I say 'some') are strong enough to cause the magician harm. If you are using a ouija to contact the dead, be sure you have a strong banishing ritual handy just in case things get out of hand. See the divination section of this book to learn what to do if a nasty spirit attaches itself to your board and won't leave. Now onto communication with the dead. One way to keep oneself 'safe' from harm during a session of necromancy is to work with the Daemons Ba'alberith, Baba'al, or Eurynomous/Euronymous in a structured ritual space. You may invoke them in a triangle if you wish, or in conjunction with the elements in an elemental circle construct if you imbalance easily. Use their Enns to invoke them as is standard in Demonolatry rites.

First, you need to make a Tincture of Ba'alberith (Mullein Tincture). You can use a spagyric tincture making method (described in The Daemonolater's Guide to Daemonic Magick) using the mullein leaves, or you can simply put Mullein leaves in some vodka and let them steep in a dark container for about a week. One part Mullein to two parts alcohol should do it. This tincture will be used to anoint the divination device and your third eye and wrist pulse points.

Keep your divination/communication device in your prepared ritual space. You should prepare your divination devices beforehand. Do not use divination devices dedicated specifically to Daemonic communication as human spirits cannot be channeled through them once they are consecrated to Daemonic communication. So keep your regular and Demonic devices separate. Your regular devices should be cleaned regularly. The Demonic ones won't need cleansing as frequently if at all.

There is no standard method to necessarily call forth a spirit of the dead. Most necromancers are natural mediums by their very nature and can contact the dead simply by calling on who they want to speak to such as:

"I call upon you [departed's name] to come forth and speak with me/us!"

Note that not being specific in who you're calling is more likely to lead to something nasty attaching itself to your communication device.

Some people say that timing for necromancy is very important. Three a.m. is allegedly when the veil between the worlds is said to be thinnest. Others insist that October 31 - November 1 is the best time of year to contact the dead. The reality is that if your medium is strong enough - (s)he should be able to perform a necromantic working at any time. For those who are still feeling their way around their own mediumship abilities, look up hourly and planetary correspondences and apply them to the timing of your necromantic work to see if it enhances your results.

I've been asked by numerous people if holding hands and contacting the dead is an accurate ritual. The truth is I've never seen a rite of necromancy performed that way except in movies. I've also seen such rites described in some old school divination and necromancy books. I see no reason why this particular method cannot be experimented with when performing a session.

Crossing Rite
Passage (To Help a Spirit Cross Over)

This ritual is specifically to help a "stranded" or resistant human spirit cross over. This can happen if the death is a suicide, violent, or sudden and unexpected. Or if the spirit just wasn't ready to cross. Keep in mind that not all trapped spirits will haunt a place or produce paranormal activity. However, a medium may still feel their presence. This particular passage ritual is a very gentle nudging to the other side. For a more forcible ritual (usually needed with more resistant or negative spirits), use an actual banishing or cleansing or contact the clergy for help. Additionally - you can modify this ritual to something stronger of your own devise.

Within a ritual space wherein is invoked Ba'alberith and Eurynomous/Euronymous by employing their enns. All those participating will carry with them one white candle and one black candle anointed with a Eurynomous oleum. The medium should be an adept magician. The medium should make contact with the spirit.

After the Daemonic forces are invoked, the medium should be able to see them. (S)He should then say,

S. Connolly

"Come close to me as I lead you to Eurynomous so that he can guide you to the other side."

The astral portal to the death realm is opened with the ZD and the invocative Enn, *"Asee Cha On Ca Ba'alberith. Anat Eurynomous!"*

Those present repeat, *"Asee Cha On Ca Ba'alberith. Anat Eurynomous!"*

The medium raises her hands above her head, *"Cross over and be at peace."*

Those present repeat, *"Cross over and be at peace."*

Once the spirit crosses the portal is sealed (see portal closing for more information). The white and black candles are left in honor of the recently departed dead at the closed portal and left to burn down. The Daemonic is not asked to leave but allowed to depart in its own time.

Attunement Rite

The following ritual is an attunement with the Death Energy and is actually quite simple to perform. It can be done within the triangle ritual construct mentioned in an earlier chapter. Sit within the triangle with your arms crossed over your chest and vibrate the Enn of the Daemonic force you want to attune yourself to. (You can chant, but vibration has a stronger effect.) If you are not getting the desired result with your arms over your chest, place your forearms on your thighs, palms facing upward. Remember that the Daemons of death are the embodiment of that death energy you are seeking to commune with. Do this for as long as you are able and close the ritual, thanking all Daemons that you invoke for the attunement. This alleviates your need to sit in graveyards to do this. Remember? I said you wouldn't have to lurk in graveyards.

That said, if you are the type who likes to hang out in cemeteries soaking in all that death energy, you can attune yourself there as well. Find a quiet spot, close your eyes, and feel the vibration move through you.

Some mediums may find this latter method particularly intense and may not be able to handle this type of attunement if they are too sensitive to the current. This does not mean you are weak or unable to handle death. On the contrary, it actually means you have a stronger connection to it. There are those who will disagree with my stance on this, and that's okay.

Honoring the Dead

This is a rite for honoring the dead. Use the triangle ritual construct invoking the Daemonic forces you wish to work with. Part the veil if and only if you wish to perform a communication session (otherwise don't). Place upon the altar a photo of the deceased.

On a piece of parchment, write all your loving hopes and prayers for your loved one. Feel free to seal it with a drop of your blood in honor of those you are honoring. Burn this in the offering bowl. Light a prayer candle and say any relevant prayers.

Perform your necromancy. Close the ritual as usual. Allow the prayer candle to burn for as long as you wish. M. Delaney had this bit of advice to offer: *Prayer candles are often burnt for seven, fourteen, or twenty one days. Each candle (white or black) is inscribed with the name of the deceased and the sigil of the Daemonic force invoked to guide the spirit on the other side.*

The Amulet of Death

Courtesy B. Morlan

This amulet helps one to connect to the death energy easier.

Using clay or wood, cut out a disc. Then carve the sigil of death (literally a sigil of the word "Death") onto it.

Anoint with your blood, and wear or carry for a month before attempting to connect to the energy.

Each day, hold it in your hands, charging it with your intent, saying: *"Manus intra obligo me tibi. Mors ades!"* which means, "Within my hands, I bind myself to thee, Death come to me!"

After the month it should be sufficiently charged and only worn when you are going to use it, or need some changes to happen in your life.

When not in use, put it in a piece of black cloth and place it under your altar close to the earth.

Changes & Starting Over

Changes can sometimes be a scary thing, as can starting over in a new place, new job, or in absence of a spouse or friendship that you've grown accustomed to. A particular ritual that caught my eye years ago and has been something I use often is the following:

Take a white clay pot and paint the sigil of Anubis on it. Anytime you feel afraid, confused or worried, write your concern on a piece of paper and toss it in the pot. Once a month, in company of Anubis, open the pot and pull out the papers one by one and read them aloud. Then, after you read each one state firmly, "I am strong and I will overcome this!" Then burn it in the offering bowl. Do this until all the papers are gone. Depending how much fear you're feeling you may choose to perform this working once a week, every other week, or even monthly.

Coping Rituals

Personal Rituals to Accept and Move Past Death

I asked a large group of people to share things that have helped them get through grief of Death and Change. Here is a smattering of some of the personal rituals people have used.

Ω

Write a letter to the deceased person. Write down your feelings (including anger and grief) and tell them how much you loved them. Write down any unanswered questions you had, and all the things you wanted to say but never did. You can either rip up the letter, bury it, burn it, throw it away, or simply pop it in the mail box with no address. Some people say this exercise helps to lift a lot of the guilt/grief/unhappiness as it releases a lot of emotions.

Ω

Others put memorial plaques on benches or trees that can be visited by grieving loved ones. A sacred space outside the cemetery so-to-speak where they can feel a closeness with that person.

Ω

Some choose to make DVD's or recordings with pictures of the deceased, and/or appropriate music to remember their loved one.

Ω

One woman said after her sister passed, she visited a beach her sister had always wanted to go to, and spread her ashes there. She said she hoped one of her loved ones would do the things she never got to do in her honor when she passed. Please note you do have to be careful of this. In most places the spreading of human ashes is prohibited and illegal.

Ω

Another woman said she and her sisters made a pledge that every time they went past the funeral home they would put their hands over their hearts and remember their grandmother. She said that helped her to remember and honor her grandmother.

Ω

Someone of Norse heritage said, "When a blood member of the clan dies, someone (Usually a young man but it can be a female too) is picked out before the funeral to be a "waiter" (one who waits). After the funeral is done this person is to go to a high point near the grave and wait there until the graveyard workers come and fill in the grave. Then they are to report back to the closest family members of the deceased that the deceased is on their way to Valhalla. Some old stories about this practice is that when members of the Norse clan were buried at sea or on water that someone would be sent to keep watch over the burning ship to ensure that the body and their things went to the bottom of the sea and that no one tried to sneak up to it and steal anything before it sank. It is now a tradition that is carried on in my family but I have never seen it anywhere else."

Ω

Other people talked about fire rituals, burning things belonging to the person lost in order to symbolically let go. Others still discussed making memory amulets for them to remember their loved ones by.

Ω

And finally – one respondent made it a point to remind us all, and wisely so, that no ritual for remembrance or to help us let go should ever hold us back from living. So sometimes it's better to let go of a ritual if it isn't helping you move on.

Coping with the Loss of a Friend or Lover
(by death of the friendship or relationship)

Loss of a relationship can be just as life changing as death of a loved one. We've all lost a good friend to a relationship gone bad. It's the nature of living. We still experience the stages of grief. Even in this particular instance we can use ritual to help us cope with, and move past a loss. Like with all death, the loss will always leave a scar.

The problem with this particular metaphoric death is that some people get stuck in the anger stage for months, even years at a time and can't move past the loss. These people end up living their lives obsessed with ex-friends and lovers (now enemies) and spend all their time obsessing over what these exes are doing. So much so that they forget to live their own lives. In instances like this – the Daemons of Death can be particularly useful to help us learn how to move forward and past the change.

I know, it's tempting, in your grief, to want to pull out the execration magick, but before you go there, hear me out. I've been on both sides of this fence. I've been the person who got dumped and I've been the person who dumped the other person. I've had the obsessive ex-friend spend years worrying about me and what I'm doing, thinking my every waking moment was spent cursing and thinking about her. Of course this was only true in this person's mind. So while my ex was obsessing over what I was doing, I was actually living my life and doing. The only person who got anything out of the years my ex spent obsessing over me was me. The ex simply fell into depression and headed into a downward, self-destructive spiral. Since we have mutual friends I'm often told how my ex is doing, but I dare not contact the ex for reasons of my own. Not to mention the ex still has it in her head that I destroyed her life by my mere exclusion of her from my life. There's a reason some relationships *have to die*. Some just aren't meant to be. This can include friendship and not just romantic relationships. So always consider this when you're trying to get over a particularly painful loss. Sometimes you're just better off without the relationship. To release yourself from the toxicity of this loss, here is the following rite.

The Rite of Release

Invoke the Daemons of Death into your ritual space. On a piece of parchment write your name and the person you wish to be detached from.

Then on another parchment write the following:

I, [your name], do hereby remove [their name] from my life! You will not hold me back. I will move on and so will you. The Daemons of Death [or insert Daemonic names directly] have severed our ties and our relationship is dead. I have no more use for you! I will rise as the Phoenix from the flames of our bitter end. I will rise. I will rise. I will rise! I release you! I release you! I release you!

Now read this aloud. Read it in a strong and vibrant voice. Read it over a second or third time if you wish.

Now say over it, **"I release you, in the name of [Daemonic force you invoked]. You are no longer a part of my life."**

Now allow the flames to consume the parchment.

Next, pick up the parchment with your name and their name upon it. Tear it in half saying, "**I have ripped our relationship asunder. It is no more!**"

Burn your name in the flames. Keep the parchment side with their name on it for later.

Close the ritual.

Next go outside, or to a graveyard if you must, and bury the parchment with their name on it.

Now walk away and let it go. Never revisit the graves of magick like this or you will only cause torture within yourself.

This is preferable to cursing because it's actually a more adult way to deal with the pain of loss of a friendship or intimate relationship. Save the energy you use on execration for those who really deserve it. Being angry just because someone no longer wanted to be your friend or lover is no reason to curse.

For those of you wanting execration magick check out both *The Complete Book of Demonolatry* or the thorough section in *The Daemonolater's Guide to Daemonic Magick*. I see no need to repeat any of that here.

S. Connolly

Banishing Ritual

The following banishing ritual was taken from an actual Daemonolatry Ritus Sacerdotal, courtesy of OFS and should ONLY be used when a spirit *won't* cross or there is haunting or poltergeist activity.

Banishment can be used to clear a space, object, or person of negative energies, or it can be used to remove negative spirits and vibrations from a place. In a sense, this is the Demonolatry version of an exorcism. Sometimes non-demonic spirits or negative residual energies can wreak havoc and cause a continued haunting or poltergeist situation. If the spirit or vibration becomes violent – a banishment must be performed.

You must always have the homeowner's permission before performing a rite like this for someone else. But chances are if you are performing such a rite – you have been asked to do so by someone else. First off, explain to the person, object owner, or homeowner what you will be doing and make sure they agree to it. Also explain that if you find an angry Demon to be the reason for the

106 | P a g e

disturbance, that you will not perform the rite (as it would be disrespectful).

If there is anything in this ritual you don't understand, please see any of the other available Demonolatry books including *The Complete Book of Demonolatry* or *The Daemonolater's Guide to Daemonic Magick* as it is assumed the reader is already versed in the methods of Daemonolatry ritual constructs and Enns of other Daemonic forces not mentioned in this book.

The Demons Called Upon via Enn:
- Satan, Amducious, and Eurynomous.

Start the rite by mixing together the salt and water and blessing it via Leviathan and Belial. Using a dagger wet with the blessed salt and water (dip into the cup before each invocation), go into each room and invoke all the elementals, Satan, Amducious, and Eurynomous. After each invocation say: **(Demon Name) Please remove this negative energy/presence from this place.**

Using a banishment incense enter each room and call out – **"Be Gone in the names of Satan, Amducious, and Eurynomous. Go back from whence you came! You may no longer dwell here and if you persist, I call upon Eurynomous to physically remove you!"**

When this step is done, use an oleum of Satan and draw the proper sigil of Satan or the DZ above each door and window saying, **"I consecrate this home in the name of Satan and the Divinities."**

If the home is a single, detached house and you can walk around it and bless the outside of the house as well.

Pay special attention to rooms where occurrences have taken place. Burn incense and black candles in those areas (supervised) and recite prayers in the infected areas.

For objects that seem to be linked with a negative energy, bury them in salt for 24 hours, and consecrate them properly afterward.

For infected Ouija boards that have not been properly prepared, they must be burned and the ashes spread into running water **unless** the board will be immediately prepared and used for Demonic workings.

For persons, anoint the forehead, temples, wrists, and ankles. Have them drink a full glass of water then go into a meditative rite for elemental balancing.

For infected places, attempt to get recordings and pictures in infected areas (contact paranormal investigators if needed) before performing the Banishment. You might better be able to know what you're dealing with.

You don't want to accidentally dispel an angry Demon with this rite if one has entered a non-Demonolator household. Chances are you can get a Demon to leave a home if you simply go into ascension and communicate with it. If the demon refuses to leave, you might try to find out why, and if absolutely necessary, ask Satan to talk to the demon and get him/her to leave. This might be the case if you're dealing with persons who practice ceremonial magick or if you are in a house or place where someone has performed ceremonial magick. An angry demon might behave like an upset spirit just to screw with the magician. In instances like this, if the persons are practicing ceremonial magick, you might suggest they stop using evocation because they're pissing off Demons.

If the person refuses to comply, and the Demon refuses to leave, don't attempt to do anything else. Simply leave.

Trust your intuition. You might be able to tell if it is a Demon, residual energy, or spirit energy you're dealing with right off. A quick jump into ascension in an infected area should tell you.

Deathly Herbals

Here are a few Deathly Herbals for your use and pleasure. These particular plants are often associated with necromancy for some reason or another. See later in the chapter for recipes.

Balm of Gilead (Jupiter) – Consecration, Necromancy, Divination, Love Magick

Frankincense – Banishing and purification

Licorice Root. (Mercury) - Lust, Passion, Fidelity, Necromancy

Mandrake – While mandrake is traditionally an aphrodisiac some necromantic formulas call for it. I only suspect this is because legend has it that mandrake uprooted from the earth lets out a death cry. Taking that a step further, the orgasm has been referred to as *the small death*. So this is the connection I'm making from it. Of course I also found this bit of lore, "The Devil regarded the plant with great favour; therefore it was associated with underground demons and other supernatural powers, and highly prized as the roots were for their magical properties, their unearthing was considered a very perilous undertaking. It necessitated a magical procedure, which was usually enacted at sunset, but occasionally in the dead of night. First, the earth was loosened for mechanical reasons, then, with the point of a two-edged sword that had never drawn blood, three circles were scratched around the plant. The magical significance attending the latter act was to prevent the demons rising with the root." *Excerpted from The Mandrake by A. Roe* I am told in this instance, by my dear friend Brid Delaney who is an avid herbalist, that the Daemonolater does not circle the plant three times before pulling it. Instead, the ZD invocation is drawn above it as the Enn for an appropriate Daemon (congruent to the purpose the mandrake will be used for) is vibrated during the process of extracting the root.

Mistletoe **(Sun)** - Protection, Love, Fertility, Healing, Necromancy

Monkshood* **(Saturn)** - Hecate Magick, Necromancy, Astral Work, Execration Magick

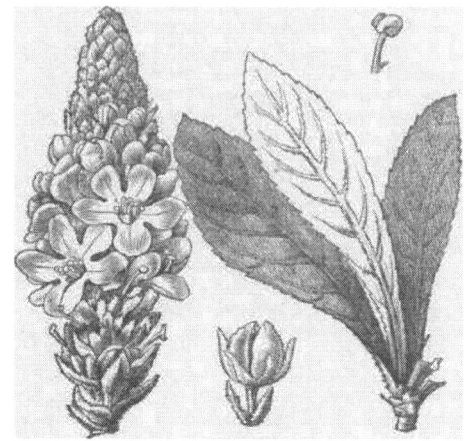

Mullein – Mullein is often called "Graveyard Dirt" and is said to increase necromantic ability. Drink in a tea before divination or sessions of necromancy for best results. Use honey with it otherwise it's kind of nasty.

Sulfur (Fire) - Protection, Execration Magick, Necromancy

White Sandalwood (Mercury) - Protection, Healing, Purification, Consecration, Necromancy

Wormwood, Organic* (Mars) - Execration Magick, Psychic Development, Necromancy, Protection, Love, Transformation

Yew (Saturn) - Necromancy, Hecate Magick, Astral Work, Execration Magick, Increases Magickal Potency

*DO NOT TAKE INTERNALLY! POISONOUS

Recipes

Baalberith Incense/Oleum – Coltsfoot, Saffron, Pau de Arco, Devils Claw, Frankincense, Solomon's Seal

Conjuring Incense – Mugwort, Wormwood, Lavender, 1 grain crushed Frankincense

Dead Gathering Incense - 1 part Pepperwort, 1 part Red Storax, two drops Musk oil, 1 pinch Saffron

Eurynomous Incense/Oleum – Cumin, Poppy, Juniper, Mandrake, Hibiscus

Exorcism/Purification – Garlic and Frankincense

Hecate Incense - 2 parts Copal, 2 parts Sandalwood, 1 ½ parts Orris root, 1 part Rose Petals or Rose Essential Oil, 1 part Cubeb Berries, ½ part Spikenard , ¼ part Nutmeg (optional) *Courtesy B. Morlan*

Mars Incense - 2 parts Galangal, 1 part Clove, a pinch Black Pepper, 1 part Coriander , 1/2 part Basil

New Beginning – 3 parts Catnip, 2 parts Orris Root, 7 parts Chamomile, 4-5 parts Damiana, 1 part Sandalwood, 4 parts Hops

Purification – 1 pinch salt, 5 parts Frankincense, 5 parts Myrrh, 6 parts blessed Thistle, 4 parts Powdered Garlic, 3 parts Benzoin Gun, 3 parts Rosemary, 2 parts Solomon's Seal, 2 parts Gum Arabic, ½ parts charcoal or salt peter

Saturn Incense - 2 parts Sandalwood, 2 parts Myrrh, 1 part Dittany of Crete, two drops Cypress oil, two drops Patchouli oil

Scorpio Incense (to heighten psychic ability) - 2 parts Frankincense, 1 part Galangal, 1 pinch Pine resin

Spirit Guide Incense – Mullein, Rue, Sage, Bay

OTHER BOOKS FROM DB Publishing

Books By Demonolators For Demonolators™

◊ Abyss: Demonolatry Hymns for Ritual & Meditation
◊ Art of Creative Magick
◊ Complete Book of Demonolatry
◊ Demonolatry Rites
◊ Goetic Demonolatry
◊ Honoring Death
◊ Meditation Journal
◊ Ritus Record Libri
◊ Satanic Clergy Manual
◊ Kasdeya Rite of Ba'al
◊ The Daemonolater's Guide to Daemonic Magick
◊ Daemonolatry on the Tube
◊ Sanctus Quattuordecim

Our books are available at Lulu, Amazon, Barnes & Noble online, and many are available for order through any bookseller. Many of our titles are also available for Kindle and Nook!

Printed in Great Britain
by Amazon.co.uk, Ltd.,
Marston Gate.